An Architecture of Dialogue

Learning from the Boulder Dushanbe Teahouse

I0202380

Edited by Katelyn Sector, Nathan Jones, and Shawhin Roudbari

With contributions by

William Bechhoefer, Sophie Burgess, Antonio Celano, Abigail Clark, Carley Cordrey, Jason Green, Grant Harrop, Ethan Herrold, Madison Liedtke, Hanaan Llewellyn, Josephine Phillips, Justice Ramos, Trevor Shelden, Madison Smith, Brett Sametz, Emelia Steinmetz, and Madison Wight.

Bäuu Press

Library of Congress Cataloging-in-Publication Data

Sector, Katelyn; Jones, Nathan; Roudbari, Shawhin
An Architecture of Dialogue: Learning from the Boulder Dushanbe Teahouse

p.cm

1. Architecture. 2. Education - Architecture. 3. Boulder - Colorado

ISBN 13: 978-1-936955-25-1

This project was made possible through the generosity of:

Community Engagement, Design
& Research Resource Center
UNIVERSITY OF COLORADO BOULDER

With contributions by:

EVOLVELAB

ETHAN HERROLD
PHOTOGRAPHY

Boulder-Dushanbe
Sister Cities

And the tremendous support of:

Three Leaf Concepts, the Boulder Dushanbe Teahouse, The Program in Environmental Design at the University of Colorado Boulder, On point Scans, and Boulder City Facilities and Asset Management (FAM).

Preface

William Bechhoefer, FAIA
Professor Emeritus of Architecture, University of Maryland

The Boulder Dushanbe Teahouse as Teacher

The Boulder Dushanbe Teahouse has become a beloved landmark and favorite rendezvous for Boulder residents and visitors. From the time of the establishment of Sister Cities ties between Dushanbe and Boulder in 1987, the Teahouse has been an ambassador from Tajikistan, testifying not only to friendship between cultures, but also to openness to ideas that are mutually enriching. Although part of a 2500-year Persian tradition of architectural and landscape design, the Teahouse has taken its place as a "citizen" of Boulder, freely offering its aesthetic and spiritual vision of paradise. And because the Teahouse is significantly located in Boulder's Civic Area, it can offer its rich array of design principles to the future of Boulder's symbolic heart.

Good buildings stimulate thinking that takes us beyond the immediate pleasure of using them. The sheer sensuous enjoyment of the light, color and space of the Teahouse might be sufficient for the casual observer. But how not to think about the craftsmanship that is so evident? And how not to wonder about the culture that sponsors the experience? And how not to appreciate and speculate about the contribution that the Teahouse makes to Boulder's urban experience?

In the University of Colorado course, "Restoring the Dushanbe Teahouse: Practices and Theories of Design Restoration, Tradition, and Cultural Identity," led by Profs. Shawhin Roudbari and Nathan Paul Jones, and Tajik restoration craftsman Marufjon Mirakhmatov, the Teahouse takes on the role of "teacher." Through hands-on restoration, students had the opportunity to be on intimate terms with the building and decorative crafts that brought the Teahouse into being.

Through graphic analysis and investigations of conceptual issues prompted by the design, students learned lessons about art, architecture and landscape that are as relevant today as they have been historically. Readers of this book may come to a greater appreciation not only of the Teahouse itself, but of the kinds of ideas that give meaning to any work of art and architecture.

Painting demonstration by Marufjon Mirakhmatov. (Photo by Ethan Herrold.)

Working with the Teahouse

Critical Perspectives

Architectural Analysis

Acknowledgments

This book principally represents the engagement between a group of Colorado design students, the Boulder Dushanbe Teahouse, and the various supporters that made this project possible. This book reflects work done as part of a design course taught in the fall semester, 2019, at the University of Colorado Boulder's Program in Environmental Design called "Restoring the Dushanbe Teahouse." The purpose of the course was to expose students to the Teahouse through its history and its architecture. The students also participated in an artistic restoration of the building's exterior walls with a Tajik master artisan. As the editors of the book, we had the privilege of facilitating bits and pieces of the project here and

Overleaf: Marufjon Mirakhmatov restoring the exterior of the Teahouse. (Photo by Kate Sector.)

there. In the process, we've learned a lot from everyone involved with the Teahouse, both past and present, and racked up deep debts of gratitude.

We offer the primary acknowledgment of the book to our visiting Tajik artist, Marufjon (Maruf) Mirakhmatov, for his friendship, his dedication, his talent, his adventurous spirit, and his enthusiasm. It has been an amazing experience watching Maruf become more comfortable in our community, learning English and new 3D modeling programs, engaging with students, and more. We treasure Maruf's friendship and impatiently await his return to begin the next project.

A monumental Central Asian teahouse would likely not be standing in Boulder were it not for the efforts of the Mirakhmatov family. We owe this wonderful family from a provincial city in Tajikistan more than we can adequately express. Haydar Mirakhmatov, Maruf's father, has committed much of his life to the preservation of the Teahouse and the artistic craft it embodies. We appreciate his diligence in assuring that this tradition persists in both Boulder and Tajikistan. Maruf's wife, Nargis, his daughters, Mohera and Mehrona, and his mother, Mavluda, spent months away from Maruf while he resided in Boulder to restore the art of the Teahouse. We sincerely appreciate their patience and steadfast support of his visit to Colorado. Finally, this book is dedicated to the miraculous work, foresight, and leadership of the late Mirpulat Mirakhmatov. Mirpulat's vision is truly what has made the Dushanbe Teahouse an icon of Central Asian artistry in Boulder.

The Program in Environmental Design (ENVD) at the University of Colorado Boulder inspired the project through encouraging creative ways of teaching and engaging architecture. With its emphasis on fostering community partnerships, the staff at ENVD leveraged its administrative tactics to make working with the Teahouse, the City, the University, and other groups possible. We appreciate the leadership of Paul Chinowsky, ENVD's director, and Alea Akins for their willingness to support such an unusual academic undertaking. We would also like to thank Paul Schroeder at ENVD's Creative Labs Center who assisted our class with studio space, materials, and heartfelt enthusiasm for the work the students carried out under Maruf's direction.

Working with large institutions such as city offices and universities is a challenging task, requiring dedicated people laboring in the trenches. Our initial challenge when beginning the project was to secure the appropriate visa for Maruf's visit (a daunting task to say the least). After spinning our wheels for months, a colleague directed us to Brian Muller, the director of the Center for Community Engagement Design and Research (CEDaR). CEDaR serves as a resource center for community engagement, urban management and design in collaboration with ENVD and other entities within and outside of the University of Colorado Boulder. After a short explanation, Brian eagerly agreed to support the project with the full arsenal of CEDaR's institutional capacity. Together with its daughter organization Metro Lab, CEDaR offered all of the logistical support necessary to organize Maruf's visit and academic affiliation. We sincerely appreciate the assistance of Brian Muller and his staff, Carmen Ardelan and Susan Glairon, whose tireless efforts made the restoration and the course that Maruf taught actually happen.

A host of individuals share the honor of facilitating the design, construction, arrival, and completion of the Teahouse in Boulder. Among these notables are former Dushanbe Mayor Maksud Ikramov, Boulder architect Vern Seieroe, former Boulder-Dushanbe Sister Cities President Mary Axe, Soviet architect Lado Shanidze, Tajik artist Manon Khaidarov, and Boulder City Design and Construction Manager Glenn Magee. We add a very special thanks to Vern Seieroe, who aided with the architectural analysis found in this book. Vern's stories, archival materials, and ambassadorship for the sister cities partnership represent the vertical axis grounding the human relationships that form the spiritual foundation of the Teahouse.

Great stories are only as good as their storytellers. The Teahouse represents an epic tale of passion, dedication, patience, and hard work. The story of the Teahouse has been authored by a collection of amazing people over the years. These storytellers include several individuals who have served on the board of Boulder-Dushanbe Sister Cities, including Sophia and Peter Stoller, Rett Ertl, Mary Hey, Joe Stepanek, David Heath, Maya Vakhobova, and Gavhar Osimi. Thank you all – your authorship has literally transformed landscapes.

William Bechhoefer, emeritus professor of Architecture at the University of Maryland, generously shared his expertly trained perspectives on the Teahouse's role in shaping Boulder. He spent time with the students of the class and challenged them to think about the character of the Teahouse with respect to its surrounding context. He helped us learn how and why the Teahouse succeeds in "being of the place" in which it is situated. Professor Bechhoefer's passion for, and deep knowledge of the architecture of Central Asia is a unique asset that all the participants in this project cherish.

The Boulder firm EvolveLAB employs a method called LiDAR scanning, which can create highly accurate 3D models of historic buildings for use in architectural restorations. The scans EvolveLAB made of the Teahouse for this project could assist with its future restorations and physical documentation. We sincerely appreciate EvolveLab's staff, Brian Juge, Cassandra Vagher, and Jake Spasaro, for scanning the Teahouse, providing a point cloud model used to create the diagrams for the book, and producing an amazing video called "The Boulder Dushanbe Teahouse Restoration Project."

Long before our Teahouse restoration project materialized, countless early morning meetings over chai took place with representatives from Boulder's Facilities and Asset Management (FAM) unit. We are especially grateful for the support, patience, and hard work of Joe Castro and Mark Simon. Their ideas, energy, and trust played an enormous role in organizing Maruf's visit to Boulder. They are the genuine stewards of our Teahouse.

The Teahouse is a popular restaurant, with customers coming and going through its doors day and night. The management and staff made a host of provisions necessary to accommodate an early morning college course and Maruf's restoration efforts. Our gratitude goes to Lenny Martinelli, owner of Three Leaf Concepts (the management group that runs the Teahouse restaurant) and his serving staff. They welcomed our band of 16 students not just as guests, but as part of the Teahouse family. Over the course of the semester, the staff indirectly guided our class through a parallel curriculum of hospitality, fine teas, and friendship. When students were working shifts on the building, they offered free meals and snacks. Through their kind assistance, we felt the honor of serving the Teahouse and its community alongside them.

Ethan Herrold, a recent ENVD graduate and participant in the teahouse course, provided the majority of photographs used in this book. We would like to thank him for graciously producing the photographic content used to narrate this book.

Peter Jones guided us through the process of editing and publishing. His willingness to take the project on through Bäuu Press and to offer flexibility with the design of the book made the experience educational and enjoyable. Our gratitude to Peter extends to independent publishers who make projects like this possible.

Finally, we wish to recognize the achievements of the 16 students involved with the course. Sophie Burgess, Tony Celano, Abigail Clark, Carley Cordrey, Jason Green, Grant Harrop, Ethan Herrold, Madison Liedtke, Hanaan Llewellyn, Josephine Phillips, Justice Ramos, Brett Sametz, Trevor Shelden, Madison Smith, Emelia Steinmetz, and Madison Wight participated in the course and contributed the essays comprising the majority of the book. They animated what was otherwise an idea for a seminar class into an engaging sequence of early morning discussions at the

Teahouse, presentations, essay drafts, studio sessions, work shifts on site, relationships, and, ultimately, these pages. They offered critical perspectives on topics in architectural history and theory and developed ways of thinking about the Teahouse that inspired debate. In the context of contemporary politics characterized by isolation, separation, and shrinking global connections, the students demonstrated the vitality of an alternative approach.

The students worked in small groups to write the book's essays. While the editors made some revisions to the students' narratives, they were mostly minimal so that the students' ideas could be expressed as they intended. When applied, our editorial hands tried to supplement some of the work the students would have done had they not been tied up with design studio reviews and final exams. The bulk of our gratitude is dedicated to their remarkable efforts.

Katelyn Sector, Nate Jones, and Shawhin Roudbari.
Summer 2019, Boulder, CO

Introduction

Nate Jones

Constructing a Trans-Global Community with the Boulder Dushanbe Teahouse

Stories, things, and the building of a trans-global community

We are disposed to identify ourselves and the people around us as a community based on the stories we share about each other. This book is a reflection of how members of a trans-global community share stories, techniques, and traditions to imagine relationships amongst people separated by generations and civilizations. The unique quality of the community in question is that its constituents reside in improbable places and are bonded through the exchange of things, long-distance relationships, and the celebration of differences. The most significant "things" representing this assemblage of individuals across continents are the gifts of monumental buildings that artists and architects designed in their homelands and sent forth to be assembled in foreign spaces.

On one side of the world is a Central Asian teahouse, entirely decontextualized from its archetypal environment–the storied urban centers associated with historical figures such as Tamerlane, Omar Khayyam, Alexander the Great, and Genghis Khan, and the agricultural landscapes of the southern Fergana Valley. Instead, this reflection of ancient Eastern craftsmanship stands amidst the green spaces of an American downtown and surrounded by the foothills of the Colorado Rockies. On the other side lies a humble modern structure that expresses a hint of Rocky Mountain architectural vernacular and placed in a residential neighborhood of a former provincial Soviet capital known mostly as the gateway to the Pamirs—one of the highest mountain ranges on earth.

It is, however, the stories that people tell each other in relation to these things—accounts shared about the design of buildings, exotic international travel, homestays with foreigners, and communication via electronic media—that endow this community with a collective identity. The stories illuminating these experiences and the actors embodying them function as the genealogical figures and mythological origins that make this trans-global community imaginable and real for its members. I stumbled into the ranks of this community that bridges the cities of Boulder and Dushanbe, the capital of Tajikistan, through sheer coincidence.

The stories and genealogies of a Central Asian teahouse

I had just started my position with the Program in Environmental Design at the University of Colorado Boulder, when a colleague came by my office and remarked that once I was settled, she would introduce me to "the Teahouse people." Having no idea what she meant by the teahouse or its people, I asked her to clarify. She explained that a Central Asian teahouse had been imported to Boulder from Tajikistan and constructed across from Central Park a few years back through the involvement of a sister cities partnership between Boulder and Dushanbe. I eventually "settled" and several months later found myself sitting down for a chai in the Teahouse with Sophia Stoller, one of the founding members of Boulder-Dushanbe Sister Cities (BDSC).

Sophia was interested in my involvement with the organization due to the rather extended amount of time I had resided in Central Asia (mainly in Kazakhstan, with some stints in Kyrgyzstan and Uzbekistan). I had never visited Tajikistan, but was familiar enough with post-Soviet Central Asian culture that she and the rest of the BDSC board figured that I might be an asset. Through this initial association with Sophia, I soon plunged into the nebulous web of individuals and things representing the stuff upon which the sister cities relationship is built. The Boulder Dushanbe Teahouse is a fascinating site, not just because of the physically iconic stature that it maintains in Boulder through its breathtaking architecture and artistic craft adorning the walls and façade. Even more enthralling is the manner by which the building has gathered people together, establishing strong and lasting relationships across continents and oceans.

Left to Right: Peter Stroller, Mirpulat Mirakhmatov, and Sophia Stroller. (Photo provided by Haydar Mirakhmatov.)

The anthropologist Katherine Verdery convincingly argues that property (whether in the form of buildings, land, or other things) serves to create relations among persons.[1] The Teahouse nicely illustrates this principle through its propensity to attract and connect people. The stated purpose of Sister Cities International, the umbrella institution overseeing sister cities partnerships in the U.S., is to support a network of citizen diplomats working to foster "bonds between people from different communities around the world." Since the inception of BDSC, the planning, construction, maintenance and operation of the Teahouse have functioned as central facilitators for establishing a vibrant sister cities community. Frequent travel to and from both countries, as well as recurrent email, telephone, and person-to-person communications between individuals in Colorado and Tajikistan (and a great deal of this international commerce occurring for purposes related to the Teahouse) have endowed the sister cities partnership with exhaustive social energy.

During our first meeting at the Teahouse, Stoller explained to me her role in establishing BDSC and the eventual arrival of a Central Asian teahouse to Boulder. Beginning in 1982, she and her colleague, Mary Hey, began organizing a committee to consider establishing a sister city partnership between Boulder and a place somewhere in the Soviet Union. At the time of this activity, Sophia coincidentally stumbled upon an article in a local newspaper announcing the wedding of University of Colorado physics professor, James Scott, and a Russian woman who had interpreted for him while he was visiting the Soviet Union. Sophia contacted Professor Scott to discuss the idea of

1.Katherine Verdery, *The Vanishing Hectare.*

establishing a sister cities relationship somewhere in the U.S.S.R. and to solicit suggestions for a possible site. Professor Scott enthusiastically responded: "I know just the city, Dushanbe."

As an initial gesture to formally recognize the new sister cities venture, the mayor of Dushanbe, Maksud Ikramov, visited Boulder in 1987 to propose immediate cultural exchanges between the two cities, including the gift of a Central Asian teahouse to function as a restaurant. In spite of this gesture, there was considerable opposition within the Boulder community to having a sister city rooted in Tajikistan, one of the southernmost republics of the Soviet Union located in largely Persian Central Asia, and a building to represent the questionable partnership. It is noteworthy that the formation of a sister city relationship with Dushanbe, the capital city of a Soviet republic, and the eventual arrival of a teahouse in Boulder represent a particular cultural moment situated in the late Cold War. Hence, understandings of the conflict between the United States and the Soviet Union largely informed the divisiveness channeling opposition to the sister city partnership and the proposed Teahouse it reflected. Ultimately, the charisma and enthusiasm of the active proponents won the community over to the prospect of partnership between Boulder and Dushanbe and the objects that would eventually represent it.

Local architect Vern Seieroe attended the Mayor's presentation to the City and remembers Ikramov's excitement about the gradual opening of the Soviet Union to the rest of the world through Gorbachev's glasnost policies. The gift of the Teahouse to Boulder was to function as the embodiment of that sentiment. Officials in Dushanbe soon identified artists from the northern Tajikistan city Khujand (then Leninabad), to handcraft the coffers, tables, and columns that constitute the Teahouse. They also designed the handsome Central Asian patterns that adorn its interior and exterior walls. Among this group was a prominent artist named Mirpulat Mirakhmatov, a master of Persian painting and woodwork. With a great deal of painstaking planning and activity, officials from Dushanbe shipped the materials that would eventually be assembled into a Teahouse for Boulder.

The pieces remained in storage until 1997 when the City finally identified a funding source to construct the pieces into a building upon the site in downtown Boulder that it currently

Mirpulat Mirakhmatov on the Teahouse roof. (Photo provided by Haydar Mirakhmatov.)

25

occupies. For this undertaking, Mirakhmatov and his Tajik colleagues traveled to Colorado to oversee its construction. As a reciprocal gesture, Boulder architect David Barrett designed a building for Tajikistan to become a "Friendship Center," expressing Colorado vernacular architecture. The Friendship Center was built in 2009 and serves as a cafe and language school located in a Dushanbe neighborhood.

Maruf's grandfather, Mirpulat, may have best captured the Teahouse's appeal in Boulder when suggesting that its purpose is "to make our souls happy."

From its ceremonial dedication in 1998 until the present, the Teahouse has embodied a moral economy encompassing (among other things) the symbolic meanings of Persian art and architecture, the exhilaration associated with the thawing relations between the United States and Russia, and the social intimacy that its current position as an iconic gathering place offers. Speaking to the stature of the Teahouse, the grandson of Mirpulat Mirakhmatov and recent visitor to Boulder, Marufjon Mirakhmatov, has said:

"In general, Central Asian carving and painting contains a centuries-old tradition, which conveys elegance and beauty in architecture. The design that we see in the Teahouse emanating from this tradition radiates positive energy, joy, spirituality, and peace. The artistic flourishes unbridle these forces precisely because they express nature, and nature is life."

Marufjon's grandfather, Mirpulat, may have best captured the Teahouse's appeal in Boulder when suggesting that its purpose is "to make our souls happy."

Stories in the making

An aspect of the Teahouse's novelty in Boulder rests in its sheer foreignness to most observers. As such, the building has made adjustments to its Colorado landscape through the acts of designers and architects. Foreign persons also make adjustments to their new surroundings, hopefully through the assistance of locals. I had the privilege of assisting Mirpulat's grandson, Marufjon (affectionately referred to as Maruf), with his initial arrival and acclimation to Boulder as a guest of the city to undertake a restoration of the Teahouse's furniture and exterior art. Maruf's first day in Colorado was emotional and exhilarating for both of us.

I had been waiting for Maruf to emerge from the international customs and immigration check point for nearly two hours at the Denver International Airport since his flight from Frankfurt had arrived. Nervous that he was being detained at the airport's Homeland Security office, I finally received a call from Maruf on my phone. He simply said, "Nate, how are you? I can't find my bag!" Soon thereafter, the 30-year-old young man emerged from the security checkpoint, and after about twenty

minutes of conversation with airline personnel, an attendant produced a suitcase wrapped entirely in plastic. Maruf grinned at me sheepishly and said, "uh-oh, I didn't recognize it." Maruf was starving after his long journey, so I took him to an Indian buffet (my nearest approximation to something resembling Central Asian food). I was, however, saving the most nourishing experience of Maruf's immersion into Boulder for an excursion after our meal.

Maruf had previously only seen the Teahouse in photographs from the periods when his deceased grandfather, Mirpulat, had resided in Boulder to participate in its construction and his father, Haydar, visited to work on a restoration of Mirpulat's work. After we finished our samosas and rice pudding, we headed downtown to Central Park, so that Maruf could see the building face to face for the first time. We approached the structure in the twilight of a late Colorado summer along a pathway through the park. From a clearing of trees, we were struck with the lights of the Teahouse, and Maruf gasped, halting to admire the structure standing before us. "What's wrong Maruf?" I asked. "You don't understand," he replied. "This is my history—this is my family. It is magnificent." Suddenly overwhelmed with the significance of the moment for this young man, I wiped tears from my cheeks as we entered the Teahouse. With his head raised and eyes wide to admire the artwork of the walls surrounding us, Maruf wandered between the restaurant's dining tables, eventually stopping to focus at one point along the ceiling with a particular inscription: Mirpulat Mirakhmatov. After a few moments of staring up at the name, Maruf gently whispered: "Grandfather, I'm here."

"This is my history—this is my family. It is magnificent."

This very recent illustration of the Teahouse's capacity to create relationships and generate stories arose through the City's need to restore the art located on the Teahouse's exterior façade and its worn furniture. Having discussed the idea of bringing a Tajik artisan to undertake the needed restorative work with City officials and Sister Cities members for over a year, we ultimately identified Maruf as the most attractive candidate. The reasons for this selection had a lot to do with genealogical legacy—Maruf's grandfather took a large part in originally designing and assembling the Teahouse and his father, Haydar Mirakhmatov, had traveled to Boulder in 2013 to undertake an earlier restoration of the building's exterior art.

Arranging for Maruf's travel and stay in Boulder was no easy feat. It required the completion of numerous applications, frequent transnational communications via email and video chats, and a great deal of frustration. In the end, with the assistance of the Program in Environmental Design (ENVD) at CU, the Center for Community Engagement, Design, and Research (CEDaR), and the City of Boulder's Facilities and Asset Management team, we successfully produced a J-1 visa invitation for Maruf's visit and work on the Teahouse. In addition to performing the restorative work on the Teahouse, we also asked Maruf to share some of the artistic techniques he had learned from his father and grandfather (and necessary for the restoration) with ENVD students as part of a college course.

The stories offered here

In the fall semester of 2018, environmental design students trained with Maruf for nearly two months to learn the painting technique necessary to apply a restoration to the north side of the Teahouse. Once the training was completed, the students assembled themselves into groups and joined Maruf on the scaffolding in shifts to undertake the sanding and reapplication of Mirpulat's original painted design. Maruf was impressed with the ENVD students' enthusiastic desire to learn the Tajik art. When discussing the experience with his students, he explained:

"According to an old expression in Tajikistan, an accomplished student should crave the discovery of knowledge. I certainly sensed a thirst to learn our Tajik painting among my design students at CU. After every lesson when I assigned homework, they eagerly accepted the challenging tasks. For example, the "spiral curl" was one of the more difficult skills I taught them. As a homework assignment, I asked the students to fill out ten sheets with the spiral repeated several times on each sheet in order to perfect their abilities to draw it. Through this difficult practice, each student managed to produce sheets of the spiral drawn very nicely and correctly. Some even filled out a few more sheets for extra practice!"

This book represents the inclusion of the sixteen newest members into the trans-global community binding together people in Colorado and Tajikistan, namely the students who

Marufjon Mirakhmatov demonstrating painting details with students. (Photo By Ethan Herrold.)

participated in Maruf's course and subsequently assisted him with the restoration work on the Teahouse. The course materials required that students train with Maruf in a studio setting to painstakingly learn the freehand painting techniques necessary to undertake the restoration. An additional dimension of the course involved seminar sessions in which students worked with Shawhin Roudbari to consider certain concepts illuminating both its historical legacy and contemporary meaning. These concepts included the nature of monuments, culture, identity, nationalism, and regionalism. The forthcoming chapters reflect

A student helping paint the teahouse. (Photo By Ethan Herrold.)

these seminar discussions, as students worked in teams to grapple with the concepts and connect them to the significance and function of the Teahouse through the course. In a sense, these essays offer new stories to further bolster this unique transglobal community with fresh perspectives, voices, and interests.

The course materials engaged the Teahouse conceptually by asking its participants to consider the building through several lenses—as an element of the Boulder built environment, a symbol of a faraway place embodying certain cultural ideals and practices, and how the structure has become incorporated into a North American cultural context. The students formed discussion groups to explore concepts related to these perspectives. We assembled the products of these discussions in a collection of student essays that constitute the following chapters. I briefly discuss the subject matter of these essays below.

The contents of our story

Enseng Ho has argued that monumental architecture possesses the force to incite discursive traditions (collective ways of communicating or understanding ideas) with the capacity to travel across space and transform landscapes.[2] These traditions are in reality the stories we tell each other about things and experiences deeply embedded within places. The Teahouse represents a monument dedicated to promoting a transregional community based on a well-established discursive tradition that began with the formation of BDSC. This discourse evokes memories related to friendship, understanding of foreign people,

2. Ho Enseng, *The Graves of Tarim.*

places and ideas, and the meaning of global citizenship. An underlying theme weaving through the students' essays is the manner by which a building inspires discourse through thought, conversation, and action with the force to make meaningful connections between people and the things that ground them.

Students of the fall 2018 class working on their essays at the Teahouse. (Photo by Shawhin Roudbari.)

In their chapter concerning monuments and memory, Burgess, Shelden, Smith, and Steinmetz suggest that monuments (including the Teahouse) may contain the symbolic force to evoke memories and emotions among its audience, inciting social connectedness and potentially building communities around collective ideals. Monuments may, however, simultaneously influence alternative meanings for its audience that go beyond shared symbols. As an illustration, the authors identify the Teahouse as a site of leisure and consumption for its visitors, many of whom are unaware or uninterested in the community-building that the site implies for others. Therefore, monuments can be experienced and interpreted creatively to suit both individual and collective needs.

Identity (in the personal or communal sense) is indeed a fluid rather than static process, and interpreting it at any stage is a slippery prospect. In their chapter on identity and place, Clark, Phillips, and Wight undertake a discussion about how certain spaces and their mutability may inform identities according to the social scale in which they express themselves (whether among individuals, groups, or entire communities). For these students, the Teahouse encourages a sense of cultural hybridity among its constituents, signaling a merger of histories and practices and influencing how one might identify with its space and by extension identify oneself. Through this process of identity-making among the local and foreign symbols of culture upon the walls and within the Teahouse, emerges the potential for the groups and individuals who consume it to imagine themselves members of a trans-global community.

Culture signifies the practices, understandings, and perspectives informing how people within a society perform social interactions. In addition to this role as a common vernacular within communities, Green, Liedtke, and Ramos view culture as possessing the connective tissue linking together people across societies with otherwise discrete habits and outlooks. They direct their attention to the schism in form and functionality inherent in the Teahouse. While showcasing Tajik art and architecture, the building serves as a site of capitalist consumption through its role as a restaurant and tourist attraction for the City of Boulder. Although engaging the Teahouse as a consumer potentially shrouds its cultural meaning in the Central Asian context, these students argue that it may also compel its visitors to find meaning with the foreign signs and symbols implicit in its structure and surroundings, diversifying a sense of culture into something that is more hybrid in nature.

As our authors suggest, identity and culture are very much grounded in locality. Embedded in the reality of local places are the forces of power that inform social practices. These forces also influence how people think of themselves as members of a collective whole—usually, as citizens of a state. Cordrey, Harrop, and Sametz consider the processes of nationalism and national identity in the context of the built environment to understand how architecture might fortify the connections between individuals and the state. The students argue that monumental architecture often exemplifies the common ideals that state citizens should collectively share. Monumental architecture may also signify a nation to its global audience. In this sense, state power is exercised through architecture. As a new state, this process has been particularly necessary for Tajikistan's leaders (and those of other Central Asian states) to fortify its position as a member of the international community. Hence, the Teahouse as a gift from Dushanbe to Boulder functions to bolster Tajikistan's national image as a legitimate sovereign nation.

"This synthesis of objective social critique and artistic practice, which the course materials and exercises endeavored to foster, is persuasively reflected in these essays."

In addition to politics, a feature of locality influencing architecture is the physical and social environments in which buildings get made. The writers of the final essay (Celano, Llewellyn, and Herrold) contend that regionalism in design reflects a social process connecting cultural identity, social change, and the natural environment. A major concern of this chapter is if the Teahouse may be considered a representative of Boulder architectural regionalism, given its iconic status for the city and the manner by which local architects transformed it to meet the City's commercial aspirations. As context for their arguments, the authors describe the traditional characteristics of regionalism found in the architectural designs of Boulder and Dushanbe. Ultimately, however, it is the social processes positioning the Teahouse in Boulder that are paramount in fashioning the City's local tradition of building a trans-global community.

Interspersed throughout the book are a series of architectural analysis pages which an ENVD student, and a member of our editorial team, Katelyn Sector, assembled as a technical illustration of the Teahouse's architectural design. These pages explore the Teahouse's features through a Central Asian and

Persian architectural lens using text, photographs, and diagrams of the building. They engage such topics as building mass, physical design features (walls, roof, and ceiling), and an illustration of the building's evolution since its original construction.

The perspectives embodied in the content of this book represent the ideas and interests of the newest members of our trans-global community, who commenced upon an intellectual and practical journey with the Teahouse's physical form and cultural legacy. The French sociologist, Pierre Bourdieu, in his *Outline of a Theory of Practice* extolled the pursuit of an intellectual inquiry into cultural practice that balances theoretical understanding with "an objectively enchanted experience of that practice."[3] I believe the work that Maruf's students undertook in his course nicely addresses Bourdieu's concern with blending an objective understanding of practice with practical experience. The students were trained in a tradition of aesthetic representation that very few designers in North America possess. I observed several training sessions in which class participants marveled at the skilled expertise Maruf applied in his teaching, as they painstakingly attempted to emulate his example. It was the experience of diligently honing artistic craft with Maruf that "enchanted" their critical thinking about the Teahouse and its meaning. This synthesis of objective social critique and artistic practice, which the course materials and exercises endeavored to foster, is persuasively reflected in these essays.

3. Pierre Bourdieu, *Outline of a Theory of Practice, 4.*

Storytellers and stewards of a trans-global community

We all gathered in the Stoller home on an early December evening to celebrate the work we had collectively accomplished in the name of the Boulder Dushanbe Teahouse. Those who were present included the students who participated in the course, members of the BDSC board, representatives from the University, a member of the teahouse staff, and others who claimed membership in our trans-global community. Maruf had prepared plov for the event—the staple of Tajik national cuisine—while others had brought various dishes to ensure we had enough food for our gathering. Our primary interest was to honor Maruf and his astounding accomplishments with the restoration and training of our students in the artistic vernacular he had learned from his father and grandfather.

Toward the end of the evening, we encouraged Maruf to stand and offer some words about his experience in Boulder. Using a little English and a lot of Russian, Maruf proceeded to thank those who had been closely involved with him during his stay. I marveled at this speech, as I listened to the young man weave together a narrative of community-building through his interactions and collaborations with everyone involved with our Teahouse project. Maruf had shared something powerful and personal with these young designers that forms the connective tissue between him, his ancestors, and his culture. He also expressed concern about how the production of the art work found in and along the Teahouse's walls is dwindling in his country and his appreciation for its preservation in a foreign place. Maruf's work in Boulder has been to fortify his story encompassing the creative soul of his family and society from which it has sprung. Regarding this point, Maruf has said:

"My father once told me when Mirpulat returned to Tajikistan after completing the Teahouse in 1998 that he wanted to teach people the national craft. I am mainly here to honor the request of my dear grandfather and conserve his life through teaching students his art."

Through sharing his skills, Maruf is placing hope in our trans-global community that we might offer stewardship over the history and identity of his family's legacy. As stewards of the stories and things constructed over the course of the sister cities relationship between Boulder and Dushanbe, we are obligated to preserve and cherish them as emblems of our regionality and anchors of our identities. To echo Maruf's sentiment as he strolled through the Teahouse for the first time in respect to our position within the legacy of the trans-global community his grandfather and others have established; "Mirpulat, we are here."

Opposite: Interior Detail. (Photo By Ethan Herrold.)

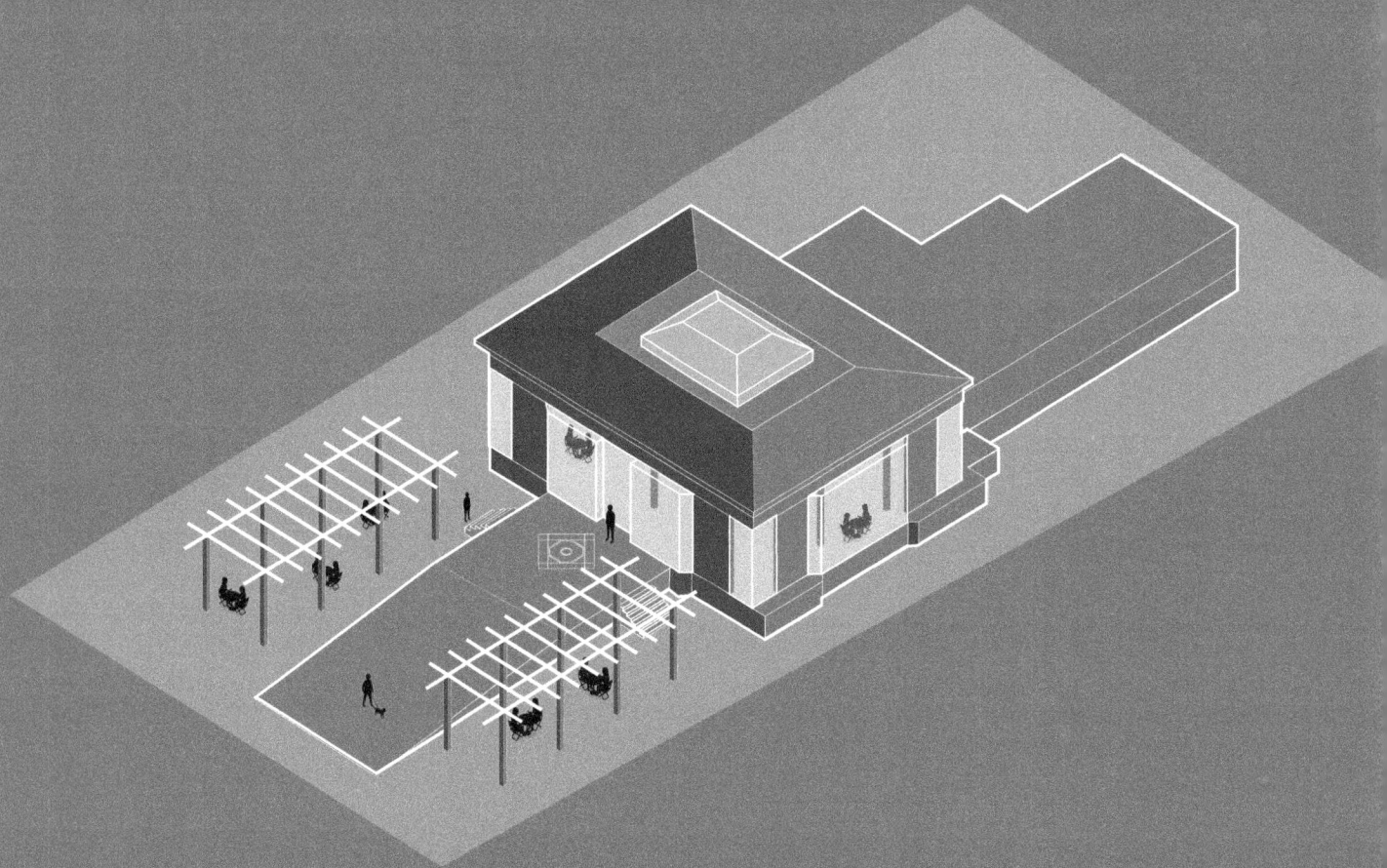

Dushanbe Teahouse axonometric view

Decoding the Teahouse

Kate Sector

The red-themed pages throughout this book support a discovery of the significance and meanings inherent in the form and details of the Teahouse. These pages summarily examine the Teahouse in the context of Boulder, the changes of the building over time, its architectural elements (such as its walls and its ceiling) through a lens of Central Asian and Persian architectural theory. Nader Ardalan and Laleh Bakhtiar's *Sense of Unity: Sufi Traditions in Persian Architecture* and Simon Unwin's *Analyzing Architecture* served as foundational texts. They are cited extensively in the analyses that follow. Interested readers are encouraged to reference those texts directly for more details not covered here.

Overview

To begin to understand the architectural significance and meanings embodied in the Boulder Dushanbe Teahouse, one can look to Persian architectural theory as a lens through which to analyze its design. Persian, as well as Central Asian, Middle Eastern, Islamic, and Sufi traditions attempt to recreate the 'cosmic of the divine' through architecture.[1] In these traditions, numbers, ornamentation, form, and color play significant roles in the design, construction, and experience of space. By understanding the spatial elements of Central Asian architecture, the significance of design choices become evident and our experience of Central Asian architecture and spaces transforms.

In Persian architectural theory, the significance of numbers add possibilities to expression of meanings and experiences through architecture. Every number has a correlating meaning that influences design decisions. An example is a cube which is regarded as a symbol of earth and the starting block of many buildings, including the form of the Teahouse. A cube is derived from the six planes and the six powers of motion in which the cube expands either up, down, front, back, left, or right to help guide the expansion of space and give a building character. Other number and geometry relations include the number three represents not only a triangle, but the three planes of the floor, walls, and ceiling, which represent, respectively, the ground, vertical transcendence, and the heavens.[2] These elements allow for an analysis of form and geometry that ultimately create and give cultural meanings to space.

1. Nader Ardalan and Laleh Bakhtiar, *Sense of Unity*, 13.

2. ibid, 27.

To begin to decorate and add character to form and space, color and ornamentation help lighten spaces and draw attention to various cosmological or spiritual meanings. Patterns and textures that "manifest the diverse qualities of creation" are commonly expressed through ornamentation. Through ornamentation, color plays an important role through its association with numbers. Seven colors make up the primary spectrum of color defined by black, white, sandalwood, red, blue, green and yellow. These colors add character to the unique ceiling and exterior tile ornamentation of the Teahouse. The seven colors correlate to the seven planets and seven days of the week and thus to the sacredness of the number seven in these architectural traditions.[3]

Using geometry, numbers, color and ornamentation to enhance the sense of architectural objects in space, these attributes draw the eye to unique characteristics of space, invoke feelings, and connect users to a greater narrative of architecture that extends beyond the building. These symbolic attributes contribute to the Teahouse's strong sense of place and intention, even when placed in the otherwise foreign setting of Boulder. These architectural techniques and their meanings have passed through numerous generations. Indeed the Teahouse continues to be part of this tradition through the participation of Tajik artists and architects in its regular restoration and repainting.

3. ibid, 73.

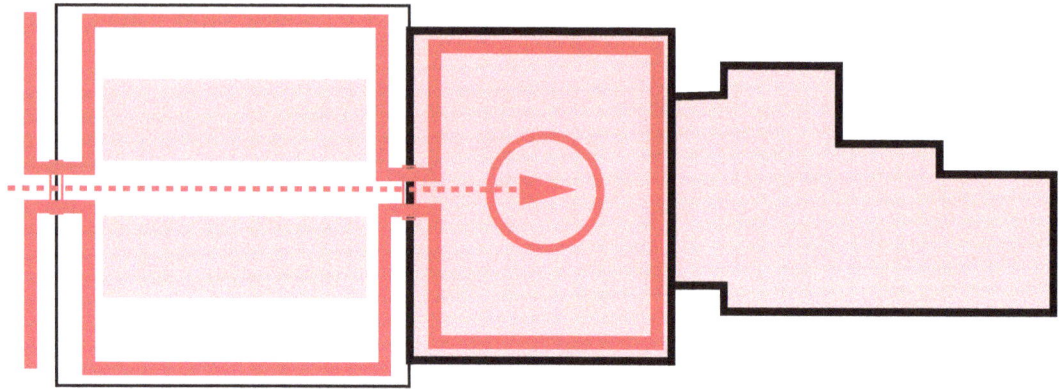

Garden   Teahouse   Addition

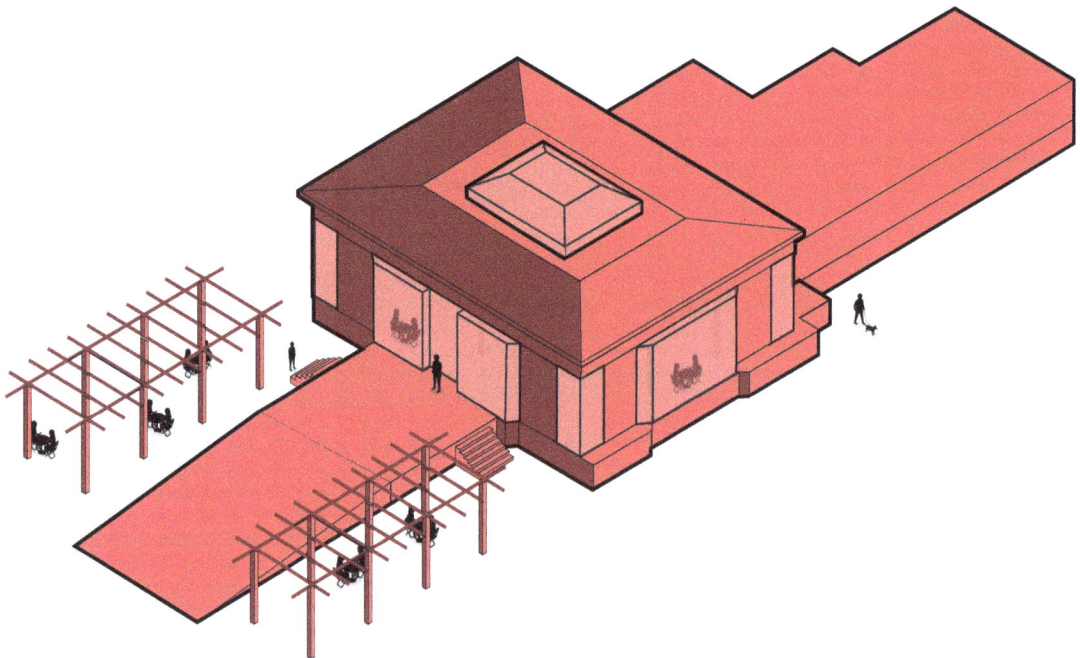

Linking Space

Connection

The gate to the Teahouse represents connection—the point at which the user's journey begins. This connecting point offers users of a space a recognizable site and sense of arrival or departure that marks a significant moment in their experience of the space.[1] Gates and openings provide a link between two spaces. Such examples can be seen in the Arc de Triomphe in France or the Tori Gates in Japan.

Transition

The pathway leading up to the Teahouse represents transition—the space between connection and culmination that draws the users attention to their destination. In addition to their independent roles, the gardens, courtyard, and pergolas guide movement by incrementally transitioning from open space to enclosure.[2] This gradual enclosing enhances the experience of exterior and interior spaces, of nature and architecture, and the connection between them.

Culmination

The interior of the Teahouse represents culmination—the space where we reside. This culmination is the final stage in the journey where users settle, enjoy, and experience the Teahouse.

1. Simon Unwin, *Analysing Architecture,* 31.

2. Nader Ardalan and Laleh Bakhtiar, *Sense of Unity,* 68.

Top: Dushanbe Teahouse floor plan highlighting connection, transition, and culmination. Bottom: Exterior axonometric view of the Boulder Dushanbe Teahouse.

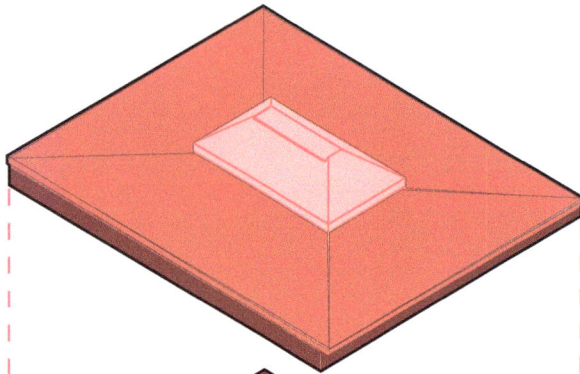

Ceiling

"The heavenly vault and the ascending arch of realization." The ceiling consists of the ornamental coffers and skylight.

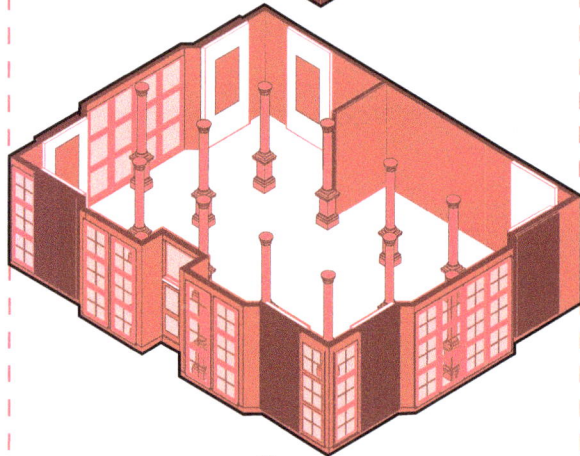

Wall

"The transcending third dimension space." The walls consist of windows, columns, painting, and more.

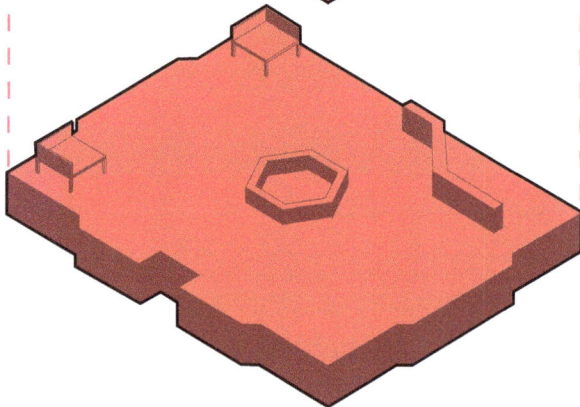

Floor

"The Earth upon which the microcosm stands." The floor consists of gardens, socle, plinths, pools and more.[1]

Creating Space

In the Persian tradition, in order to create space, it can go beyond the basic creation of floor, wall, and ceiling, and be enveloped in three levels of embellished surface: each surface resembles an opportunity for the transcending qualities of material choice, ornamentation, and positive form. Interior design through ornamentation show that surfaces themselves have a sense of place, that contribute to enhancing the overall creation and personality of a space by, for example, encouraging reflection and heightened presence within a space.[2]

Ceilings, walls, and floors allow the building to seek expression and have a sense of outward expansion. These elements of Teahouse will be analyzed in turn. Indeed, every major surface in the Teahouse has a distinct purpose. The following pages highlight their unique character, history, and influence within the Teahouse.

1. Nader Ardalan and Laleh Bakhtiar, *Sense of Unity*, 35.

2. ibid, 35.

Interior of the Teahouse. (Photo by Ethan Herrold.)

Monuments and Collective Memory

Sophie Burgess | Trevor Shelden | Madison Smith | Emelia Steinmetz

Have you ever had the chance to skip across the colorful stones of Ludbreg's 'Center of the world' in Croatia, and stand at what was once believed to be the very nucleus of it all? Or perhaps you've been lucky enough to stand before 'The Witches Well' in Edinburgh, Scotland, and imagined the accused of the 15th century being burned at the stake in the very cast iron fountain standing before you. Chances are, you've never even heard of these places, or considered their existence. And yet, there they stand, embodying the collective memories of the people in their communities, establishing significant historical events, places, and people, and commemorating a communal train of thought. These types of symbols are present all over the world, in every society. These are our monuments. Our defining societal features, the epitome of what we find culturally significant. These relics are important to our communities, and directly signify our ideals. Monuments evoke emotion and create memorable places for our societies.

...embodying the collective memories of the people in their communities, establishing significant historical events, places, and people, and commemorating a communal train of thought.

1. Monument (n.).
Online Etymology
Dictionary.

How does a monument represent memory and emotion through marking a time in history? The word "monument" contains the Latin root "mon-" which means to remind or warn.[1] Memory is significantly tied to the meaning and definition of monuments. Meanwhile, the dictionary's definition of a monument is, "a statue, building, or other structure erected to commemorate a famous or notable person or event." This definition focuses in more on the form of monuments, and seems to argue that monuments need to be man made entities constructed for a specific purpose. However, Achim Timmermann, the author of *Memory and Redemption*, has a more encompassing, fluid definition of monuments that combines both of these ideas. He defines monuments as "a demarcation in time that allows us to remember a specific event through the form of which that memorial takes."[2] This definition focuses on both memory and

2. Achim Timmer-
mann, *Memory and
Redemption*, viii.

form, and allows us to expand our traditional ideas of monuments to recognize these characteristics in multiple places and structures beyond what we have been told to consider. There is an understanding in this definition that the form of a monument can be adaptable, which is important as it suggests an expansion of the dictionary definition that can be varied based on different cases. In this sense, when we define monuments we must understand how they directly relate to the outstanding memory a structure or place can have on both individuals and groups.

Monuments hold significant meaning throughout the world and across societies. They are crucial in characterizing our connection to memory and place. James Osborne describes monuments as exuding "inherent fragility of memory," and that memory differs for everyone.[3] Users are affected in different ways by the same monument. The Boulder-Dushanbe Teahouse is a unique example of this connection to memory; it is a traditional structure that has been gifted by one country and adopted by a foreign one. While the Teahouse may not reflect the traditional values of its current geographical location, it has become a monument for the people of Boulder. In a sense the Teahouse is a foreign piece of architecture to the Boulder landscape. Its forms of intricate detail and fine craftsmanship are found nowhere else in Boulder, which allows the user to question where it came from and why. In learning where it originated, we understand its history and share some of the memories that come with it. In *A Companion to Public Art*, Cher Krause Knight, defines monuments as having significance in a community and calling attention to the landscape around them.[4]

3. James Osborne, "Counter-Monumentality and the Vulnerability of Memory."

4. Cher Krause Knight, *A Companion to Public Art*.

The Teahouse, adopted by the Boulder community, serves as a significant piece within the town's patchwork.

Monuments evoke emotion, both positive and negative, that mark important periods in time. Large, classical monuments are often times a statement and mark a time in history that is important. According to Quentin Stevens, they are affirmative of events that have occurred.[5] These are also typically what we envision when we think of the word "monument." This perception, however, begs clarification for the interpretation of smaller, more personal monuments. Are these objects disqualified from the classification of being a monument because they are unconventional, or do they still count for their significance for a collective memory, place, or purpose? How, then, should the Teahouse be classified? By traditional definitions,

5. Quentin Stevens, et. al. "Counter-Monuments."

Aerial view of the Teahouse and surrounding area. (Photo by Sam Veucasovic.)

monuments spark an emotional reaction to a historical event. How can the Teahouse, which is more personal through its interactions and sense of place, become a place of memory? One thing that seems to reveal itself when exploring this question is that the definition of a monument is subject to change depending on the situation, time, and place. Although a monument has different meanings depending on the situation, there is no singular, direct answer, only a set of guidelines that can be translated into a criteria.

Since monuments act as markers for specific periods in time, they become tools with which societies can measure growth.[6] Monuments open up a realm for criticism on certain viewpoints and whether or not society has grown as a whole. This carries a sense of importance because it allows collective views to be challenged by the masses, creating a chance for them to change.[7] Monuments are a necessary part of our world because they allow us to reflect on our past and see how far we have, or have not, come. We feel that opening and challenging such views is essential for our social formations.

Monuments and landmarks seem very similar, but in some ways, they can be very contrasting. Both are usually built objects that hold significance for a group of people. Both stand out and can be recognized from multiple places. Monuments hold a higher cultural context compared to landmarks as they more often represent a belief or feeling rather than a location. As Edwin Heathcote describes in his work, monuments hold a certain level of memory, inducing powerful feelings among those it impacts.[8] Landmarks, like the Pearl Street Mall in

6. Quentin Stevens, et. al. "Counter-Monuments."

7. James Osborne, "Counter-Monumentality and the Vulnerability of Memory."

8. Edwin Heathcote, *Monument Builders*.

Boulder, act more as objects to help one navigate through a city or atop a mountain, while a monument makes you stop and feel something on a deeper level.[9]

As globalization proceeds and tourism rises, the interpretation of monuments evolves. Rather than being created solely to represent a certain set of ideals by a population, monuments have now transcended, becoming a tool for capitalism and consumption. Monuments are marketed towards travelers as interesting, important destinations that can often be coveted more for their aesthetic value than their underlying purpose. Some locations, like the Teahouse, survive off of this consumption, and entire industries are built on the success of this type of tourism. The Teahouse was built on the agreement of making it more consumer based than its original form has taken. It needed

Teahouse interior.
(Photo by Ethan Herrold.)

to become a restaurant to create a strong attraction as a way to weave this foreign idea into the culture of Boulder. This capitalistic cycle of production and consumption can be both positive and negative. Take the Colosseum or the city of Pompeii, the businesses and livelihoods of workers around them survive off the profit made from tourists. Yet the sheer amount of people who visit these places everyday may be degrading in the long run. Some feel that such commercial consumption is illegitimate or even unethical, defeating the purpose of certain monuments. In their eyes, tourists do not understand the importance of a monument like the Egyptian pyramids. Others feel this increase in consumption is important for both production purposes and the spread of certain ideologies. In either case, it is clear that the way in which we interpret monuments is changing, which may or may not change the definition of monuments inherently.

Another contrasting aspect monuments have is size and form. Landmarks tend to be large, built structures while monuments can range in size and can be natural or man made. Landmarks are purely functional and are created for a specific purpose but monuments contain "a strong overtone of symbolism" and this symbolism can vary depending on the person or group of people.[10] Perspective matters.

Monuments allow us to look back to certain events or periods that have significance in history. They place a stamp on a specific moment for future remembrance. Visiting them either reminds or educates people on what came before. One could classify all monuments as monumental because they strike a

10. Thomas H. Creighton, *The Architecture of Monuments.*

feeling of awe and allow people to ponder their existence. But something could be monumental without being a monument, such as a large building or beautiful piece of artwork. With a beautifully painted facade and incredibly intricate interior the Teahouse sets the perfect example of how structures can be monumental without showing dominance through size. The Teahouse space holds a finite amount of people and creates an atmosphere that inspires remembrance and emotions. Even the small details hold great meaning, but may seem small in comparison to large classic monuments.

Monuments can mean much to some and little to others. The impact a place can have on individuals and groups can drastically define what a monument is. In "Counter-Monumentality and the Vulnerability of Memory", Osborne states that, "to some people it represents a time they are prideful about, but to others it brings up memories of conflict and hurt."[11] Consider Mount Rushmore. To many it is thought as a dedication to North America's founding fathers, and is an act of respect and homage. However, to the Sioux and Cheyenne on the Black Hills in South Dakota, the American monument is a desecration of a site sacred to their heritage and culture. Marc Treib, a historian of modernity and monuments in architecture argues, "whether intended or not, architecture and designed landscapes serve as grand mnemonic devices that record and transmit vital aspects of culture and history" showing truly how much word of mouth can generate power across cultures.[12] With the power of memory and monuments, memory distortion, the difference between what actually occurred and how one perceives an event, becomes a prominent factor in the history of any culture.

The idea that memory is temporary has radically changed in the past decade because of technology.[13] Social media, photographs, and videos can have a large influence on how we interact with monuments today. We experienced this with the Teahouse this semester. After posting photographs and a few videos of the Teahouse, multiple colleagues and friends have reached out to us saying that they have never been to or even heard of the Teahouse. After explaining the interaction we and the rest of Boulder's community have with the

11. James Osborne, "Counter-Monumentality and the Vulnerability of Memory."

12. Marc Treib, *Spatial Recall.*

13. Andreas Huyssen."Monument and Memory in a Postmodern Age."

Teahouse on a weekly basis, and the work we have been doing, these peers not only visit it now but have also brought guests back to the Teahouse as a result of it becoming one of their "favorite" buildings in Boulder.

Memory can come from more than just personal experience. People are able to connect with a broader range of monuments all around the world without ever physically visiting them. We argue that the definition of a monument is a fluid, adaptable set of criteria including emotional significance, a strong tie to history, collective memory, and a range of forms. This criteria is subject to change as societies and their values are altered. For the most part, monuments of today work to project certain ideologies and values which relate to both physical place and collective memory. These factors are dependent on how consumers relate to both the monument itself and its context. The Teahouse is a monument to the people and cities of Dushanbe and Boulder, as it represents both a higher thought and a specific cultural relativity. Although different from the normal buildings and structures found in Boulder, the Teahouse adds a specific cultural outlook in which Boulderites can be a part of and create memories. Monuments also mark the growth of society, or lack thereof. Sometimes, we need reminders of the past to push us towards a greater future. Monuments are that reminder.

Opposite: Teahouse sign. (Photo by Ethan Herrold.)

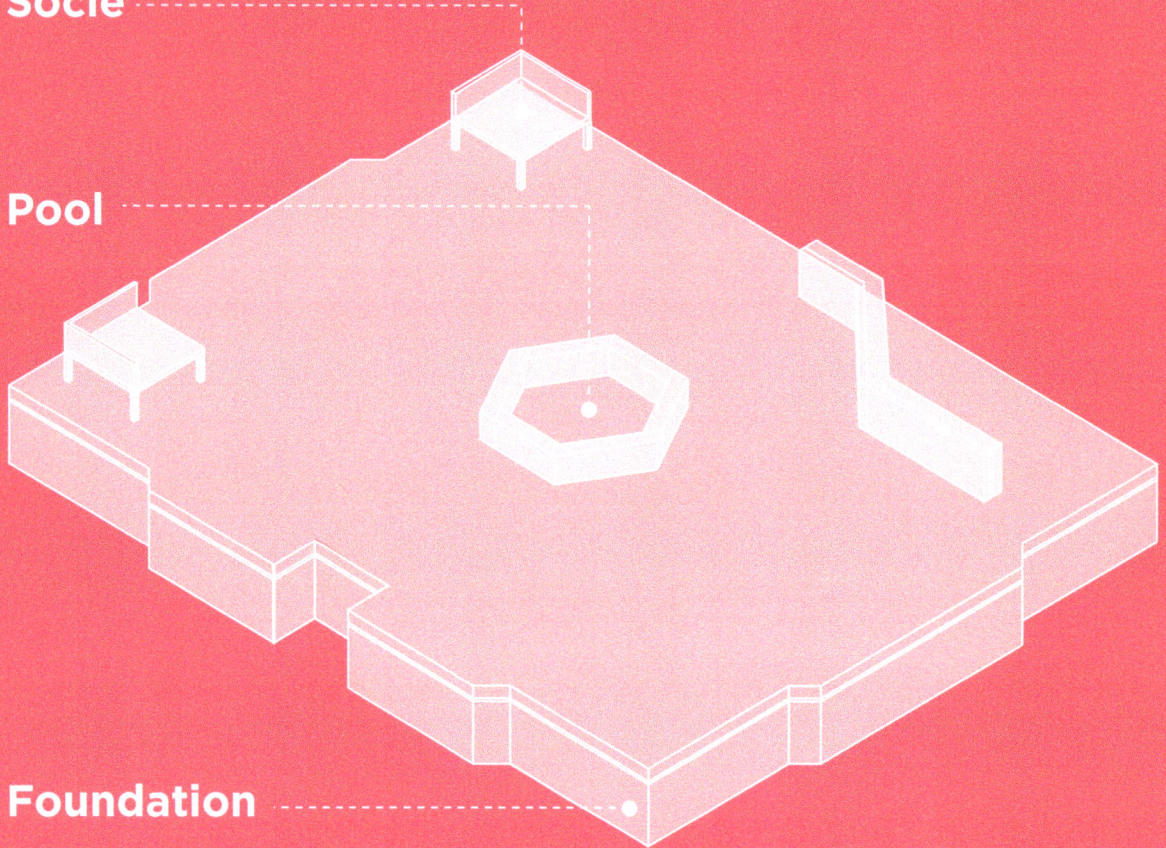

Socle

Pool

Foundation

Dushanbe Teahouse interior floor axonometric view

Floor

The floor is the first step in creating space. It represents the horizontal dimension that symbolizes the "earth upon which the microcosm stands."[1] Furniture and other spatial elements emphasize the horizontal elements of the floor through lines and patterns, but do not distract from other components in the walls and ceiling. The floor encompasses gardens, socles (raised platforms), and pools.

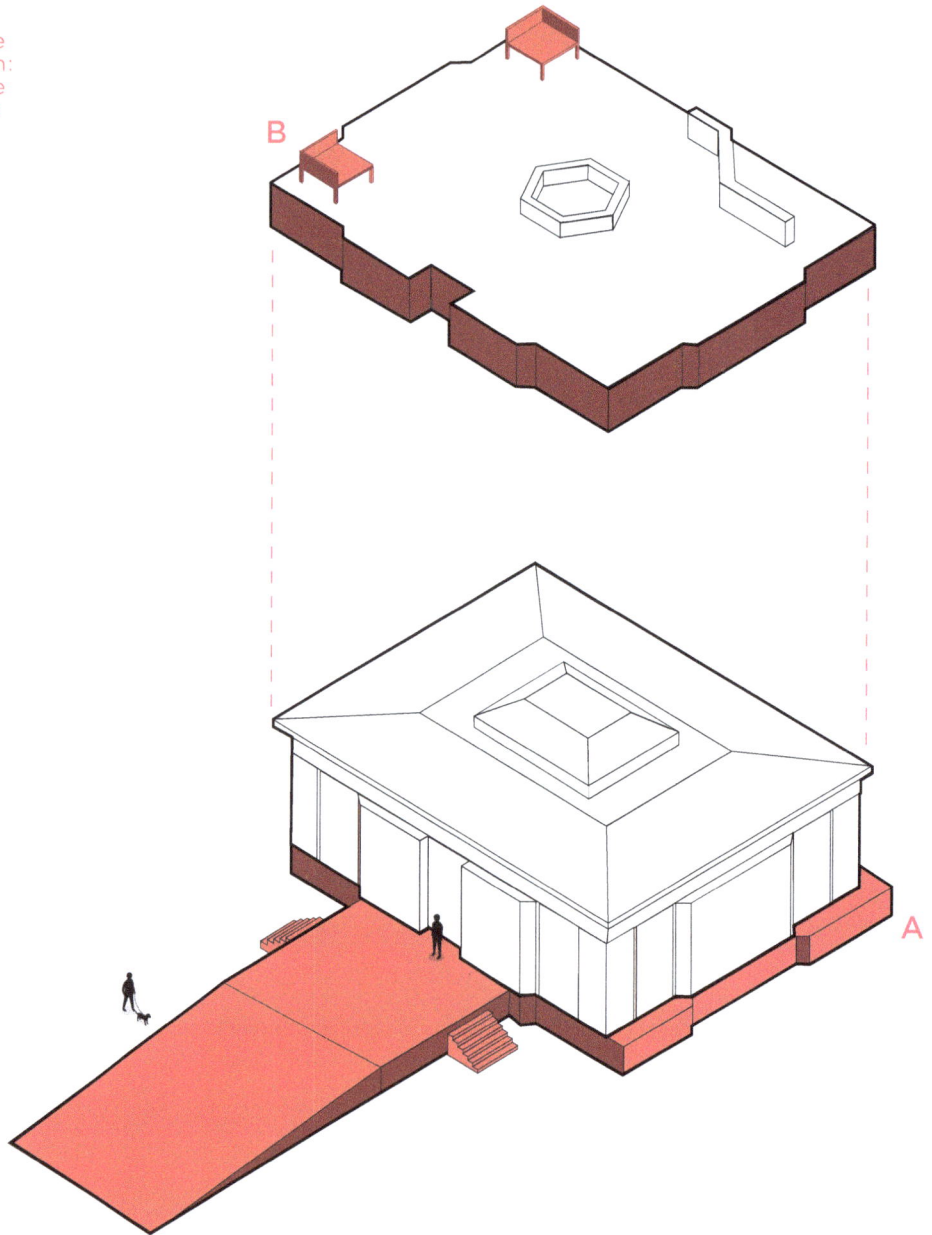

Top: Two socles inside the Teahouse (labeled B). Bottom: Dushanbe Teahouse exterior foundation axonometric view (labeled A).

B

A

Foundation + Socle

The foundation (Labeled A) is the first floor element that grounds the Teahouse. The original design was a traditional raised foundation, which renders the ceiling visible to visitors from the exterior when looking through the windows. Due to the creek nearby, this element became even more crucial to locate the ground of the Teahouse at an elevation that would minimize flood risk.[2]

In the Persian tradition a socle (Labeled B), is a raised platform or surface. These elevated spaces draw inspiration from mountains or other high places that are often sites of sacred relics.[3] This element is present in the Teahouse as represented by the two tapchana (or raised platforms) placed in the corners, colorfully painted and decorated with ornamentation and pillows.

1. Nader Ardalan and Laleh Bakhtiar, *Sense of Unity*, 35.

2. Personal Interview with Vern Seieroe, Fall 2019

3. Nader Ardalan and Laleh Bakhtiar, *Sense of Unity*, 68.

Raised bed in the Teahouse. (Photo by Ethan Herrold.)

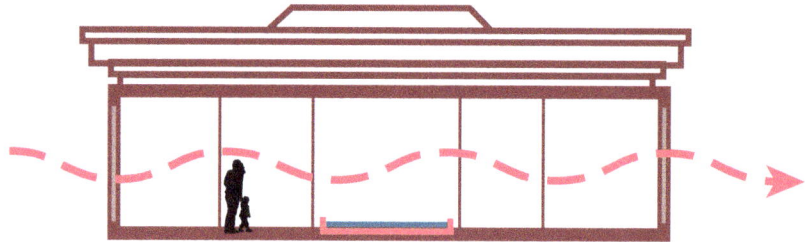

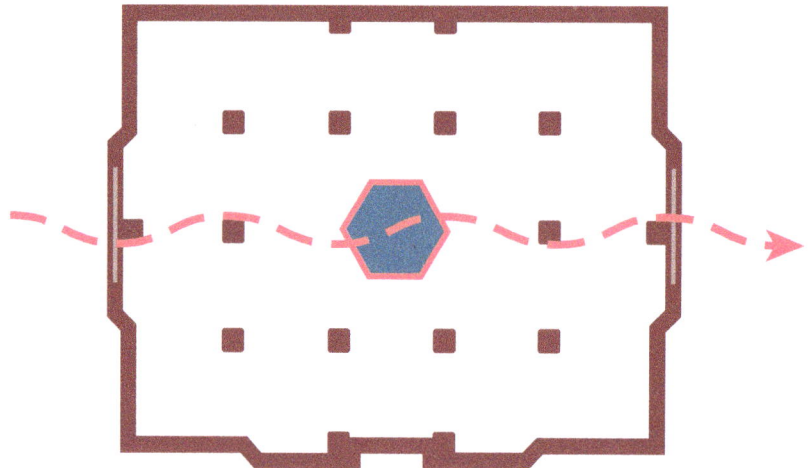

Top: Original interior section showing airflow. Middle: Modified interior section. Bottom: Interior floor plan.

Pool

The original design is an open plan with a lowered pool that allows for wind to better cool the space. Air flows over the pond, evaporating water, and circulating cooler temperature through the space. In addition, pools, due to their mirror-like qualities, symbolize heaven reflecting itself upon the earth, which serves to unite the floor with the ceiling and create space.[1] In order to comply with The Americans with Disabilities Act (ADA) to prevent discrimination of those with disabilities, and Boulder's climate, walls were added and the pool was raised. The pool can still serve the purpose of cooling the Teahouse's interior when the front door is open and when windows are opened to allow a breeze to pass into the building.[2]

1. Nader Ardalan and Laleh Bakhtiar, *Sense of Unity*, 35.

2. Personal Interview with Vern Seieroe, Fall 2019

Statues in the Boulder Dushanbe Teahouse pool. (Photo by Ethan Herrold.)

Culture as Connection

Jason Green | Madison Liedtke | Justice Ramos

Picture yourself standing beneath a blue sky, the clouds tinted with crimson from the sunrise. The break in the landscape that was caused by jagged silhouettes now begin to reveal themselves to be mountains towering above the city that you're within. The city itself is surrounded by nature and built from a red brick veneer complimented by the sandstone from the surrounding area. Among the brick veneer and sandstone masonry resides a building that distinguishes itself from the rest. Vibrant paintings cover the facade of the building and immediately catch your eye. The procession leading up to the building begins with a low-set black gate. Once you're beyond the gate there is a long walk up to the building that is infused with a deep aroma drifting through the air. The red and white roses are the beginning of the lavish garden that surrounds you. On both sides, two identical canopies of tall vines stand above the rose bushes. Visitors are sitting beneath laughing while enjoying tea and a small meal. Beyond the garden you're reminded of the impressive structure that excited your curiosity. The building is simple but grand. The detail and craft are what set it apart from any architecture you have seen before. Once you're through the orthogonal entryway your breath is taken away. For a moment you're overwhelmed by the paintings that encompass everything within. The ceiling is screaming with detail and color. Even the pillars are carved with a craftsmanship unmatched by anything you've seen before. As you continue to a seat you admire the hexagonal fountain that resides in the middle of the building. Would you believe you're in Boulder, Colorado? The Teahouse becomes a link between cultures. Some qualities fight for control while others work together to create something completely new.

To begin to understand these spaces and their implications, viewing the world through a cultural lens offers insight. Culture, although a very broad term, can be simply defined as the "spirit of a people."[1] In other words, the essence or combination of fundamental values that begins to define the lives we live. Edward B. Tylor, an English anthropologist writing in the late 19th century, describes culture as a "complex whole which includes knowledge, belief, art, morals, law, custom and any other capabilities and habits acquired by man as a member of society."[2] Culture is comprised of things we create, learn or share when working together.

1. Finn Neilsen,
"AnthroBase"

2. Edward B. Tylor,
Anthropology.

Architects use ideas about culture to better understand spaces. The way a space is used is affected by the culture of a society and therefore the purpose begins to be defined by that culture. Architect Amos Rapoport writes, "house form is not simply the result of physical forces on any single causal factor but is the consequence of a whole range of socio-cultural factors seen in their broadest terms."[3] He argues that "what finally decides the form of a dwelling, and molds the spaces and their relationships, is the vision that people have of the ideal life."[4]

3. Amos Rapoport, House, Form and Culture, 47.

4. ibid.

Architecture is the combination of the physical form it possesses and the function that it holds.

Architecture is the combination of the physical form it possesses and the function that it holds. Homes are developed by people who live in them and how they choose to lay them out. A vision of an ideal life is a major factor in what shapes the built environment. This vision is portrayed through the values and morals of societies. From these values, connections between the culture and the architecture of a society start to form. The Teahouse has influences from American and Tajik cultures. The cultures, morals, and values of each can be observed from the built form but they retain an added complexity through the combination of the two cultures. (See the discussion on the evolution of the Teahouse in the red-themed pages, for example.)

Consider the traditional Japanese home as a vivid example of the architectural legibility of cultural practices. The traditional Japanese home is defined by characteristics of the house such as the shoji screens, Tokonoma, and the entrance hall. Self-control is shown through the limited amount of privacy the house grants the residents through shoji screens. They are constantly aware of others in the house and how their actions affect others. Honor is represented through the Tokonoma or decorated alcoves used to remember their ancestors. It is the honored and sacred place in the room often holding important and valuable artwork.[5]

5. Jiro Jarada and C. Geoffrey Holme, *The Lesson of Japanese Architecture*.

The traditional Japanese home is defined by characteristics of the house such as the shoji screens, Tokonoma, and the entrance hall. (Photo from homedit.com.)

Culture in architecture is also expressed in practices and customs. The practice of pilgrimage greatly influences architecture in Tajikistan. This influence is created from the importance placed on monuments within pilgrimage sites.

The Dushanbe capitol complex shows this influence. The monumentality created by the buildings begin to evoke a feeling from "walking around national monuments [that] in some way approaches pilgrims' practices during ziyorat (pilgrimage)."[6] This is also evident in the Teahouse. While it is not a large building by any means there is a processional experience created by the architecture. See the Overview section of the red-themed pages.) The Teahouse becomes something more than a restaurant.

In our thinking about architecture and culture, we debated how and to what extent the Teahouse is an accurate representation of Tajik culture. In his work on globalization in architecture, Ibrahim Mostafa Eldemery writes, "the tension between anti-global and pro-global forces has long existed, with two opposing forces affecting architectural globalization. One force seeks to safeguard and promulgate established indigenous architectural traditions, forms, decorative motifs, and technologies. It advocates historical continuity, cultural diversity, and preservation of identity, all symbolized by a particular architectural vocabulary, just as spoken languages and local dialects impart identity. The other force promotes invention and dissemination of new forms using new technologies and materials in response to changing functional needs and sensibilities."[7] Before technology and new means of communication, people were not sharing architectural styles and cultures with one another at the pace and scale they are today. Each was distinct from one another due in large part to the fact that travel was less frequent, and communication more limited. Globalization may be homogenizing architecture around the world.

6. Katherine Hughes, "From the Achaemenids to the Somoni."

7. Ibrahim Mostafa Eldemery, "Globalization Challenges in Architecture."

8. Ibrahim Mostafa
Eldemery, "Global-
ization Challenges in
Architecture."

9. World Trade Press,
Tajikistan Society &
Culture Complete
Report.

Because of this, it is frequently the case that some architecture is no longer distinguished by place. Eldemery also notes that, "for some, globalization entails the Westernization of the world. Some see globalization as generating increasing homogeneity, while others see it producing diversity and heterogeneity through increased hybridization."[8] Globalization affects the built environment by both standardizing it and making it more diverse.

We ask then, how is the globalization of architecture and culture affecting the Teahouse? And how are American and Tajik cultures expressed in the Teahouse? The consumer-oriented operation of the Teahouse competes with the traditional sense of its design. In Tajik teahouses, hospitality is emphasized over consumerism, and a sense of welcome is much more prevalent within the Tajik Teahouse.[9] In its operation in Boulder, we argue that the Teahouse is an "Americanized" version of a Tajik teahouse.

(Perhaps uncomfortably, we liken this view of the Teahouse to how foreign countries mark their McDonald's restaurants with their own cultural modifications.) It is possible, or maybe even likely, that the for some, Tajik culture is manifest in the Teahouse as decorations that serve to attract us to consume the Teahouse's commercial offerings without engaging in the many other Tajik cultural experiences the Teahouse offers. Architecturally speaking, Tajik culture is expressed through the building's form and ornamentation but isn't directly express it through its function. This may be attributed to its displacement from its traditional setting. Indeed, Harold Proshansky reminds us that, "there is no physical setting that is not also a social, cultural, and psychological setting."[10]

Cultural hybridity becomes a helpful framework for thinking about the Teahouse. Political scientist Nomar Nedim helped us think about how all culture has been influenced by one another, therefore making all cultures a hybrid.[11] Through interacting with the Teahouse in our discussions, our restoration work, and the community that participates in the Teahouse, we feel that the Teahouse is exemplary of architectural cultural hybridity in creating a hybrid of Tajik and North American culture. If the Teahouse romanticizes Tajik culture while also serving as a space for implementing Americans' cultural events such as weddings, parties, classes, and holiday celebrations it is addressing more than just one specific culture. What does this mean for the Teahouse? As a work of architecture then, the Teahouse offers our society a unique opportunity. Cultural hybridity introduces diversity. In some cases it compels Teahouse visitors to think about their daily practices and cultures.

10. Harold Proshansky, "The City and Self-Identity."

11. Nedim Nomer, "Ziya Gokalp's Idea of Cultural Hybridity."

The Teahouse is but one example of the change the world is experiencing. The identity of many spaces is defined by more than a single culture. Countries and cultures coexist in new ways. Architecture bears witness to this. In rare cases, architecture facilitates this. Understanding the opportunities for cultural hybridity is the key to developing a new perspective on how people interact with each other and the built environment. Humans are innately social and through these social tendencies ideas spread. Cultural hybridity is becoming a new norm and creating distinct spaces like the Teahouse will become the framework for the interaction of cultures for generations to come.

Farmers market outside the Teahouse. Opposite: Customers enjoying dinner at the Boulder Dushanbe Teahouse. (Photos by Kate Sector.)

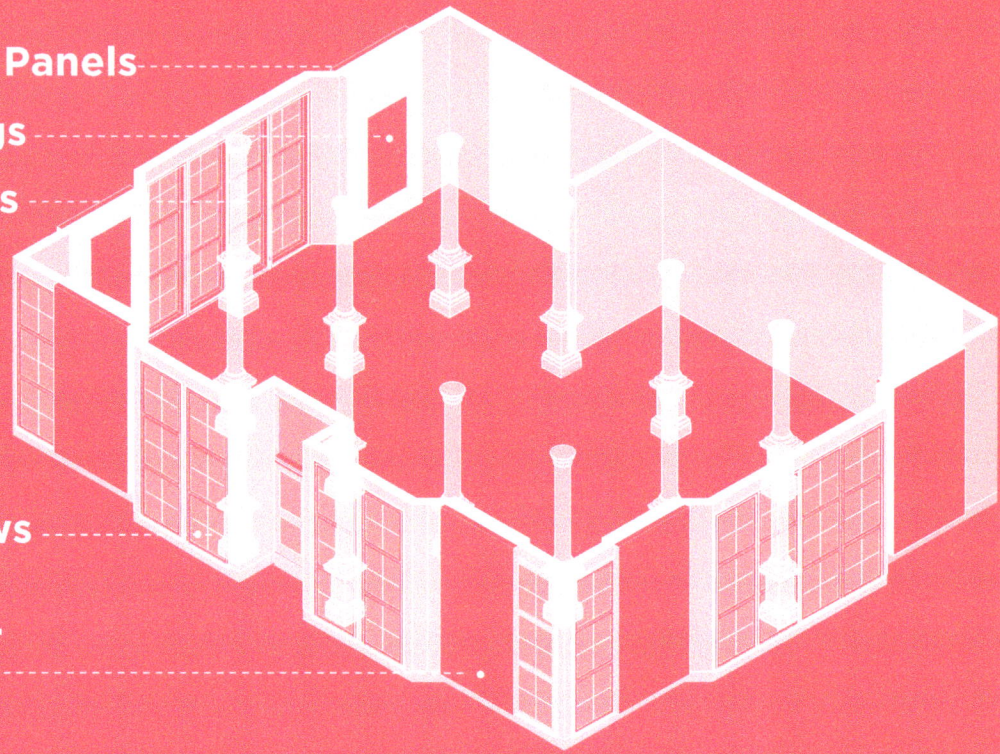

Interior Panels

Paintings

Columns

Windows

Exterior Panels

Dushanbe Teahouse interior wall axonometric view

Wall

Walls, columns, and other vertical elements represent a transcendence into the third dimension of space.[1] In architecture, walls and columns are typically the structural systems that transfer the weight of the roof to the ground (walls also help resist lateral loads from such forces as wind, retained soil, and earthquakes).[2] But walls serve more than a structural function. They are an opportunity to improve space through embellishment. This is typically done by adding positive space through convoluted and concave carvings to give the illusion of expanded vertical space, allowing for the room to feel more open and light. Tiled panels and paintings added to the walls have a similar effect.

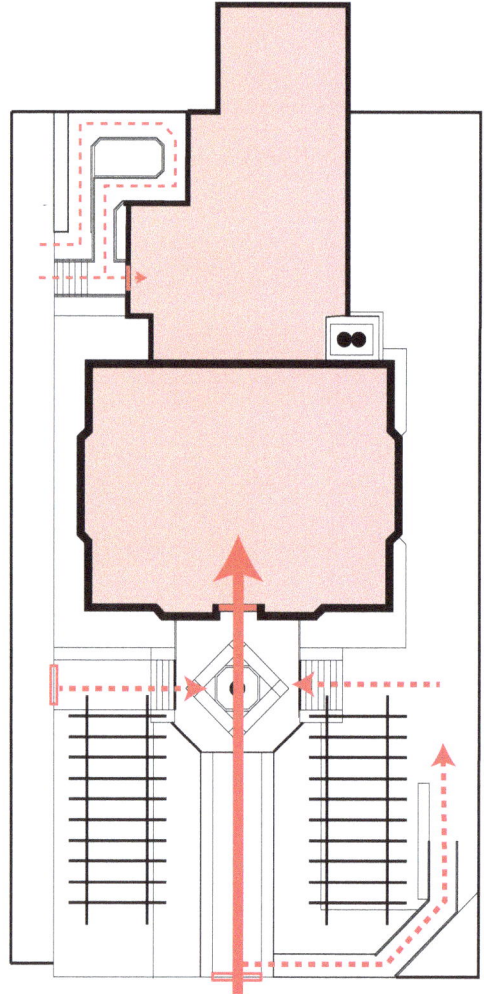

Entrance

The original Teahouse design had no doors.[3] The structure was meant to be an open-air pavilion. Openings or gates, such as the entrance of a cave, imply a sense of passage from one space to another and are an important concept in the physical transition through space. In the case of the Teahouse, however, a front door was added to the original design for security and climate control. The recession of the doors and their centrality on the access of transition situates them to still serve the purpose as a transitional space into the Teahouse.

1. Nader Ardalan and Laleh Bakhtiar, *Sense of Unity,* 37.

2. Simon Unwin, *Analysing Architecture,* 52.

3. Personal Interview with Vern Seieroe, Fall 2019.

Original front elevation concept for the Boulder-Dushanbe Teahouse by Lado Shanidze, 1988. Opposite: Entrance concept comparison; Teahouse floor plan and circulation. (Image from BDSC archives.)

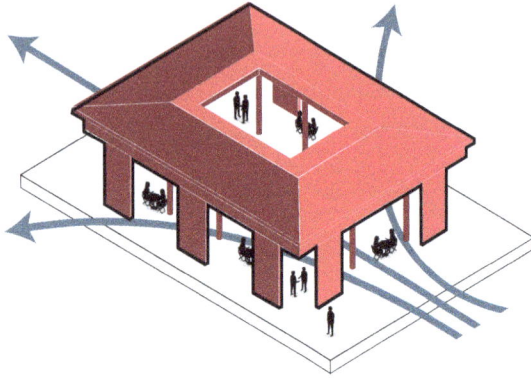

Original Teahouse Design Airflow

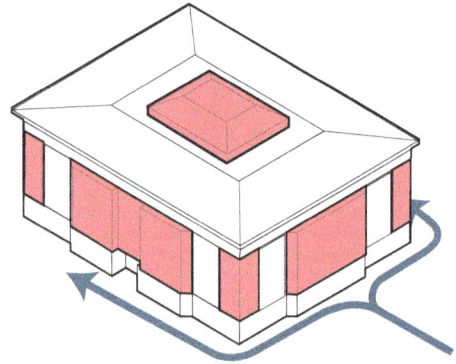

Window Addition

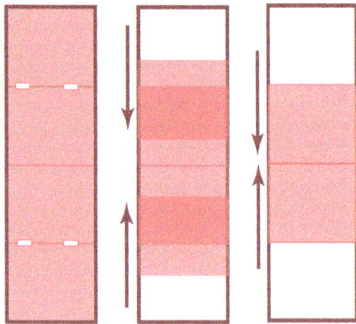

Custom Window Design

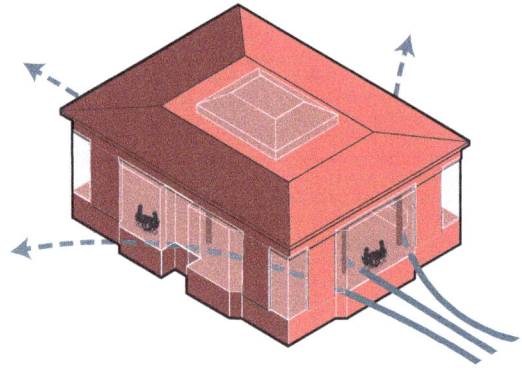

Resembles Original Design Airflow

Series showing the
original Teahouse
window design
compared to
today's design.

Windows

When the Teahouse was first designed, there were no windows in the design, only the tiled panels, roof, and supporting columns. The traditional design was meant to be an open outdoor venue with abundant views and mostly unobstructed airflow. However, given Boulder's climate and safety requirements, the designers decided to install walls and windows to provide an enclosed space. Seieroe however, wanted the design to maintain the original intent as an outdoor space.[1] In order to do this, he designed the windows to be operable from both the top and bottom in order to allow for passive ventilation and swamp cooling methods (a method that uses water-soaked pads to cool the air) during the summer.[2] Despite its nature as a fully enclosed space, this thoughtful intervention allows the building to maintain key original design intents.

1. Personal interview with Vern Seieroe, Fall 2019.

2. Jeff Flowers, "Evaporative Coolers".

Teahouse windows. (Photo by Kate Sector.)

83

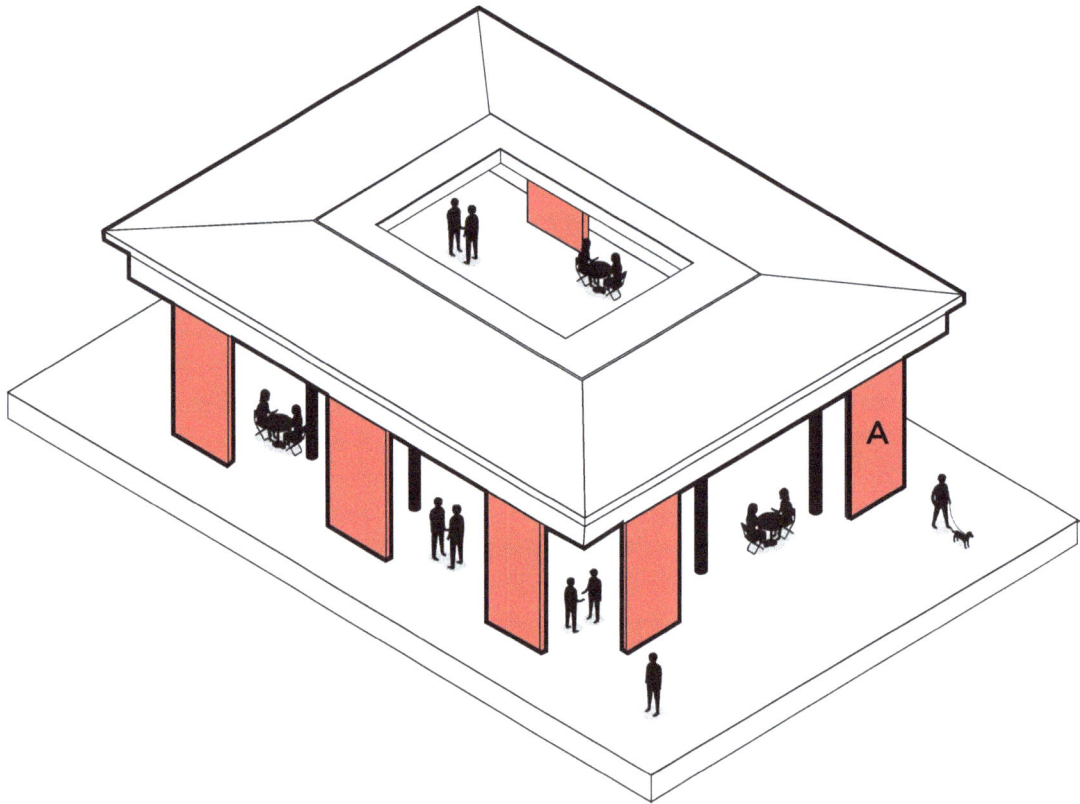

Exterior Walls

The original wall design was an open-air pavilion made up of the brick, plaster, and tile panel walls before the designers added windows and doors.

Exterior Tile Panels

There are eight custom ceramic panels (labeled A) that surround the exterior of the Teahouse, creating its colorful facade. The tiles were designed by Victor Zabolotnikov, a Tajik artist, who traveled to the United States from Dushanbe to apply them to the exterior in 1998.[1] Various stories can be found illustrated on each panel through Persian and Tajik plant and animal motifs that are framed around a niche.

1. Lara Ramsey and Kathryn Barth, *Boulder-Dushanbe Teahouse. Boulder, Colorado, 15.*

Ceramic tile detail. (Photo by Ethan Herrold.) Opposite: Original wall configuration.

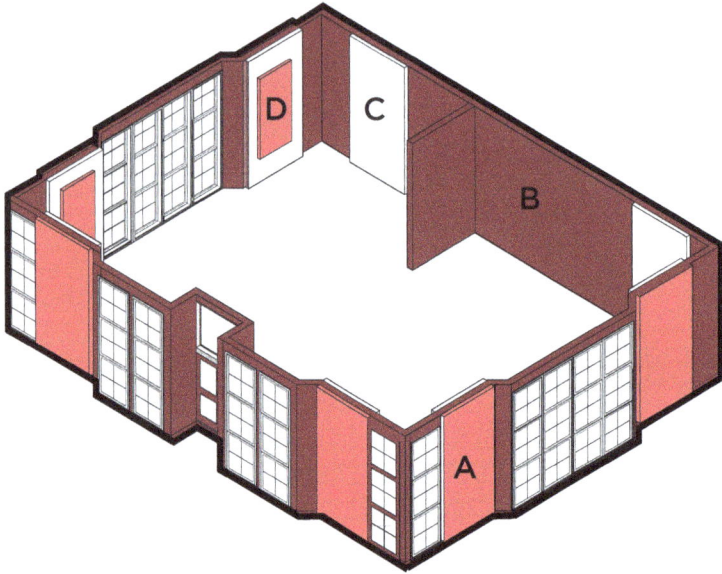

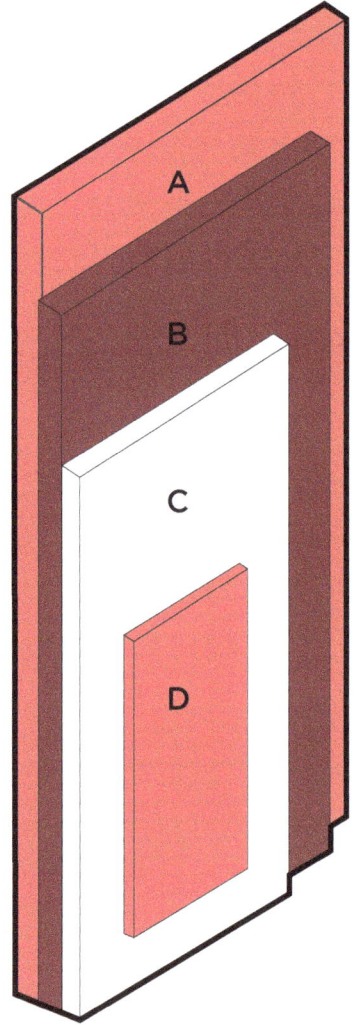

C

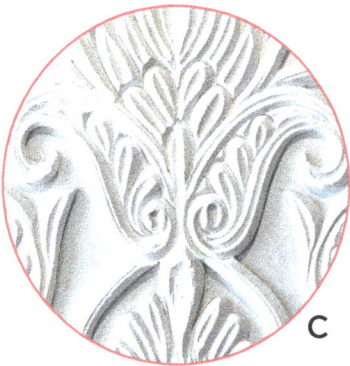

D

Interior Walls

Interior plaster panel

Inside the Teahouse are eight carved white plaster panels (Labeled c) placed on the brick walls (Labeled B) with motifs of leaves, flowers, and other natural forms created by Kodir Rakhimov during his original visit to Boulder. Motifs like these, carved into plaster "draw attention away from subjective interpretation and place all art into the realm of eternal."[1] Plaster thus offers a medium through which to carve out positive space and add character to architecture by enhancing surfaces. Phrases such as, "open hearts overcome differences" are carved within these panels as didactic architectural expression.

Paintings

Immersed within the plaster and brick layered walls are four oil paintings (Labeled D) that were painted by Rakhimov. Traditionally, most Teahouses in Dushanbe have oil paintings hung on the walls depicting nature and animal motifs.[2] When the Tajik designers consulted with Boulder architect Vern Seieroe regarding what type of paintings the Teahouse should have, they decided to incorporate a mix of Soviet and Persian art to accurately reflect the period in which the struggle to realize the Teahouse took place.

Opposite: Current wall configuration; wall detail; interior plaster panel detail; Right: paintings. (Photos by Ethan Herrold.)

1. Nader Ardalan and Laleh Bakhtiar, *Sense of Unity*, 33.

2. George Peknik, *The Meaning of the Boulder-Dushanbe Teahouse*, 16.

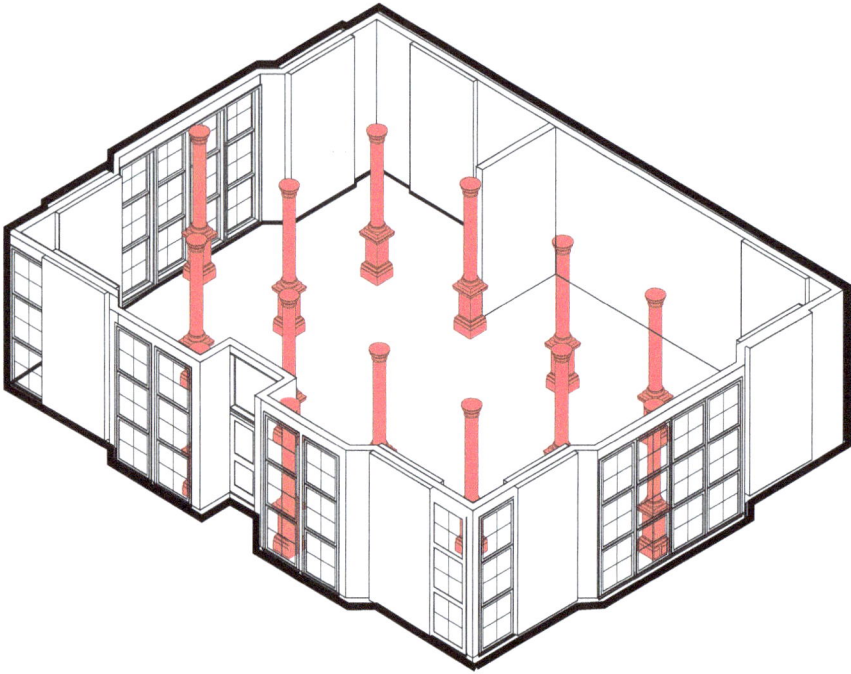

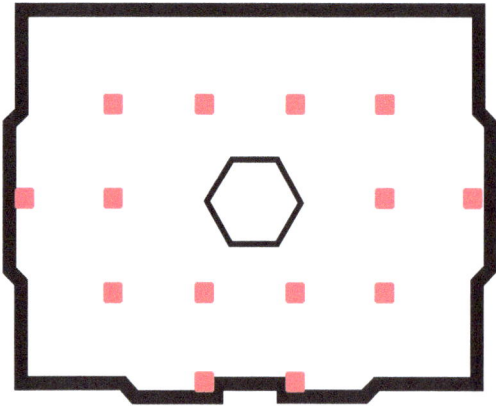

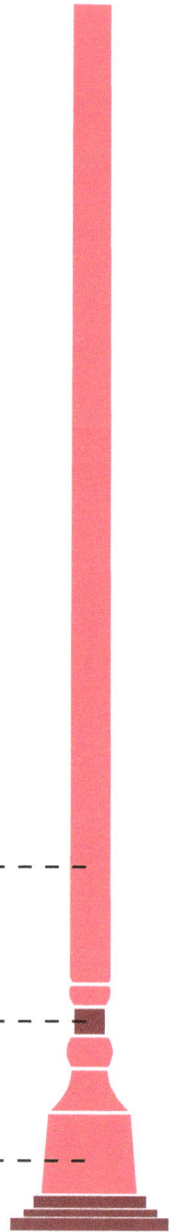

Wood Shaft

Joint

Wood Base

88 Wall

Columns

Columns of wood throughout history were used as additional structural elements within buildings before modern day columns that use iron, steel, or concrete. A unique characteristic of the teahouse is that it uses wood columns, fashioned from two trees, connected with a metal joint.[1] The designers placed fourteen evenly spaced columns in the Teahouse to resemble a grove of trees.[2] Each column is unique with floral, vine, and leaf motifs carved out of wood with a steel core.

1. Personal Interview with Vern Seieroe, Fall 2019.

2. George Peknik, *The Meaning of the Boulder-Dushanbe Teahouse*, 14.

Wood column detail. (Photo by Ethan Herrold.) Opposite: Axonometric highlighting grove of columns; floor plan highlighting column locations; column components.

Identity Reflected in Place

Abby Clark | Josephine Phillips | Madison Wight

The places that surround us affect our identity and we in turn reflect our identity in the places around us. The relationship between identity and place has many layers—and it is constantly affected by culture, personality, social constructs, globalization, history, and tradition. For example, the identity of the Teahouse has influences from both Tajik culture and the culture of Boulder (national identity, in particular is further discussed in the following chapter). The architecture itself reflects Tajik identity through the use of symbols, but the use and program of the space reflects the identity of Boulder and general Western cultures of commodification, recreation, and cultural consumption.

Overleaf: Boulder
Dushanbe Teahouse
interior. (Photo by
Ethan Herrold.)

1. "Identity." In Inter-
national Encyclopedia
of the Social Sciences,
2nd.

2. Charles Correa,
"Quest for Identity."

3. Ibid.

4. Åshild Lappegard
Hauge, "Identity and
Place."

The International Encyclopedia of the Social Sciences defines identity as "the overall character or personality of an individual or group."[1] Personal identity is how a person individually differs from people while social identity is how people relate to others. Our focus is on how identity is affected by place, in both the personal frame and the broader social frame. Charles Correa, an acclaimed architect and activist from India, links architecture to culture by articulating identity as a process that is not simply found at one moment in time, but acts as a trail made "by civilization as it moves through history. The trail is the culture, or identity, of that civilization."[2] He goes further to say, "identity cannot be fabricated. We develop our identity by tackling what we perceive to be our real problems."[3] Upon this foundation of identity, we consider how theories of global identity, conflict in identity, and hybrid identity bear upon our understanding of the Dushanbe Teahouse.

Åshild Lappegard Hauge, an environmental psychologist, defines three theories that provide a useful framework for discussing identity in the context of the built environment. She starts with place-identity theory, which "has been described as the individual's incorporation of place into the larger concept of self."[4] Place identity theory says our physical environment has an impact on our identity and self-perception. When asking people to describe themselves they typically start with where they are from. This shows how place is a prominent part of their identity. Where we are from impacts the kind of environment we want to be in and how we identify ourselves. Someone can describe themself as a city person because they grew up in a city.

They then begin to identify with characteristics or traits that are part of "city people," such as enjoying being around people or socializing in certain ways. Places affect how we see ourselves. In turn, places are influenced by people's identities. Decorating a room or apartment with your belongings help you identify more with the place. That place becomes a part of your identity and represents you. This creates 'place attachment' which "is defined as the feelings we develop towards places that are highly familiar to us."[5] They become part of our identity because we feel a strong connection to those places. For example, a Boulder local could develop place attachment for the Teahouse if they regularly visit and have memories of family gatherings there. The place has meaning to them because it has become part of their identity. Tajik natives who live in the Boulder area can also feel a close connection to the Teahouse because it

5. Ibid.

Marufjon Mirakhmatov studying the interior of the Teahouse. (Photo by Kate Sector.)

represents Tajik culture and cultural heritage. The reason we connect with places can be drastically different between two individuals.

Hauge also describes social identity theory, which associates place with a group, lifestyle or social status and contribute to their identity. People are attracted to places that increase their self-esteem and avoid places that negatively impact their self-esteem. When you are in a group there is a certain dynamic or identity of your group that attracts you to certain places where the group's identity is welcomed and encouraged. In the broader sense, group identity applies to cultural identity. Hauge quotes Breakwell, a social psychologist, who says, "in Western industrialized cultures, Breakwell... sees the current guiding principles as continuity, distinctiveness, self-efficacy and self-esteem."[6] These guiding principles affect the identity of Western cultures and also affect our architecture.

The final theory Hauge describes is the identity-process theory—the idea that we identify with places because they contain symbols that have meaning and significance to us that have been developed over time. Places represent personal memories to the individual, shared memories to the group, and shared histories to cultures. The biggest difference in this theory versus place identity and social identity is the concept of time. The meaning of places are constantly changing and "their contribution to identity is never the same."[7] New and different places impact our identity either through "attenuation and accentuation" or "threat and dislocation." Over time we either continue to identify with a place or no longer identify and feel the need

6. Åshild Lappegård Hauge, "Identity and Place."

7. ibid.

to leave. Just as we are constantly changing, so are the places in which we live. When living in one place for a long period of time, we often adapt to its changes. Being an active member of creating those changes, roots your own identity in that place. "Places are not only contexts or backdrops, but also an integral part of identity. Even small architectural changes affect how a place facilitates different uses or attributes, such as social inter-action, which thereby can also alter the meaning of a place."[8]

8. Ashild Lappegard Hauge, "Identity and Place."

"Places represent personal memories to the individual, shared memories to the group, and shared histories to cultures."
-Åshild Lappegard Hauge

A series of design strategies were theorized by architecture theorists Geoffrey Broadbent and later Yasser Mahgoub. These strategies that define the extent to which architects gravitate to traditional architecture, modern architecture, and places in between. There is the pragmatic design strategy that is akin to copying traditional architecture. The iconic design strategy uses traditional architectural elements but produces new building functions. The analogical design strategy attempts to resemble traditional architecture, but without using its traditional elements. The canonic design strategy applies principles of traditional architecture without copying its shapes or elements.[9] The symbolic design strategy reinterprets traditional architecture, while avoiding obvious traditional elements.

9. Geoffrey Broadbent, *Design in Architecture.*

10. Yasser Mahgoub, "Architecture and the expression of cultural identity in Kuwait."

And finally, the metaphoric design strategy is farthest from traditional architecture, it creates dramatic experiences of the contemporary cultural identity of a city.[10] These design strategies help us understand the extent to which a building resembles its traditional architecture and identity. For us, the Teahouse would most closely fall under the pragmatic design strategy as its form copies that of the traditional teahouse architecture of Tajikistan, with relatively minor differences being the closed ceiling and walls, a door at the entrance, and the internal furnishings that help the space function as a restaurant.

What we see happening in Denver connects to Charles Correa's theory, that, "we find our identity by understanding ourselves, and our environment. Any attempt to short circuit this process of understanding, or to fabricate an identity, would be dangerous to us all."[11] Denver, trying to fabricate a new identity for the city, has endangered the original identity of the area and created this conflict between the new and old identities.

11. Correa, "Quest for Identity."

A building can have more than one identity. The Pantheon in Rome is an example of this. This relic was once part of the Roman Empire and then during the fall of the Roman Empire this temple was transformed into a Catholic Church.[12] The Pantheon is still a functional Catholic church that holds mass every week. Most people don't know this because the commercial reputation of it is a Roman Relic.[13] Tourism has fundamentally changed the meaning of this iconic structure. Nevertheless, the Pantheon is a hybrid version of what it once was. The Teahouse similarly represents an identity made hybrid by tourism. It's identity and Boulder's have, one could argue, merged.

12. Ernest Renan and Charles Beard, *Lectures on the Influence of the Institutions.*

13. Mark Cartwright, "Pantheon," Ancient History Encyclopedia.

Hybrid identity can be successful when the intent is to preserve a cultural identity. This is seen in museums through the act of collecting symbols and artifacts to preserve a culture and its identity. The National Museum of African American History and Culture in Washington, DC does this by placing a piece of architecture representative of African American culture on the National Mall. The museum is clad in "bronze plates perforated with patterns that reference the history of African American craftsmanship."[14] The building won Design of the Year in 2017 where competition judge David Rowan is quoted saying, "in the context of today's strident American debate on race and identity, Adjaye's achievement represented optimism."[15] The Museum represents the identity of African American culture. The building embodies a hybrid identity.

14. Alice Morby, "Adjaye's African American History Museum."

15. Alice Morby, "Adjaye's African American History Museum."

The National Museum of African American History and Culture in Washington, DC. (Photo by Alan Karchmer from nmaahc. si.edu)

With some of these ideas about identity in mind, we return to the questions asked at the beginning of this chapter. Where are you sitting right now? Do you identify with this place?

There are many layers of identity that may define the place you are inhabiting right now; whether it be culture, traditions, social constructs, or some manifestation of globalization. These layers have been created by us and they shape our physical surroundings. The relationship between personal identity, social identity, cultural identity, and our physical surroundings is cyclical and evolves through time. The Teahouse is affected by these layers of identity. Tajik culture created its architecture through a pragmatic design strategy while we adapted the program to the culture of Boulder. Preserving shared histories not only preserves culture, but also the identity that has shaped what a building has become. To forget a history, therefore, is to forget our own identity and what makes us who we are.

Opposite: Marufjon Mirakhmatov restoring the exterior paintings. (Photo by Kate Sector.)

Axonometric view of the Teahouse highlighting the roof components

Ceiling

A final element in defining a space is the ceiling and roof. In Central Asian traditions, domes and coffered roofs represent the cosmic vault and the "ascending arch of realization."[1] The vaulted ceiling is traditionally decorated with intricate ornamentation and patterns that help transform a flat surface into one that expands the sense of space and draws one's eyes upwards and connects the individual to the sky, heavens, or cosmos. Many architectural landmarks across Central Asia have intricate domes or coffered ceilings that serve as centerpieces of the spatial experience. These themes can be seen as an evolution of the prototypical spheres mounted on cubes in ancient Persian architecture, which represented the coming together of the cosmic and earthly domains.

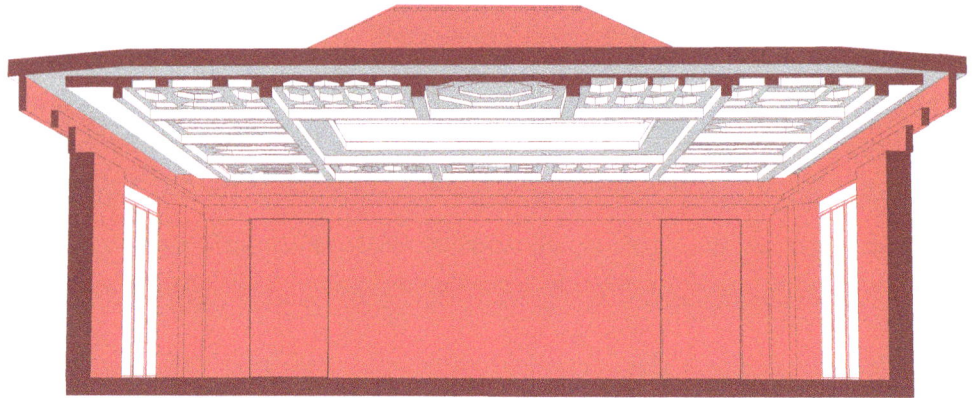

Top: Section per-
spective rendering
of coffers. Bottom:
Reflected ceiling
plan.

Coffers

The ceiling and coffered design represent the "cosmic house" that Persian architectural traditions associated with the heavens. Coffered volumes and ornamentation attempt to lighten mundane ceilings through patterns and colors as well as the addition of volume. This design strategy not only alludes to the heavens, but suggests a physical "container" of space. In the case of a traditional dome, the decorated ceiling draws viewers to individual and center point above them, as if looking up into a star-filled night sky. With the fourteen coffers in the teahouse, this strategy is replicated and repeated within multiple coffers in a larger space.

1. Nader Ardalan and Laleh Bakhtiar, *Sense of Unity*, 37.

Ornamental coffers at the Boulder Dushanbe Teahouse. (Photo by Ethan Herrold.)

Color plays a significant role in adding depth and character to the coffers. There are seven colors, known as the palette of *haft rang*, that make up the primary spectrum: black, white, sandalwood, red, blue, green and yellow. [4] These contrasting colors, as well as combinations of them, are evident in the decorative paintings on the coffers, enhancing the intensity of each color and draw the gaze upward.

4. ibid, 48.

SUMMER SOLSTICE (73 degree) at noon

FALL/SPRING EQUINOX (50 degrees) at noon

WINTER SOLSTICE (26 degrees) at noon

Daylighting

SKYLIGHTS

Originally, the Teahouse was designed to have an opening in the roof to let in light and increase ventilation. Modifications were necessary to keep the same daylighting effect while also sealing the space to make it compatible as a conditioned space in Colorado's climate. To achieve that intent, a large skylight was designed to bring light into the center of the space. The effect is abundant natural light, illumination of the painted interior, and an emphasis of the upward movement of the gaze.[1]

1. Personal interview with Vern Seieroe, fall 2019.

Teahouse Skylight. (Photo by Ethan Herrold.) Opposite: Daylighting diagrams

DAYLIGHTING DIAGRAMS

Due to do the skylights, orientation, and additional windows in the Teahouse, its interior offers a very well lit room. The diagrams illustrate one example of how the space is illuminated by daylight at noon throughout varying seasons highlighted in red.

National Identities of the Teahouse

Carley Cordrey | Grant Harrop | Brett Sametz

Architecture provides more than a place of refuge. It encompasses the identity of a nation, and in some cases, multiple nations. The Boulder Dushanbe Teahouse stands as a unique example of how architecture does not have to be limited to a single national identity through its engagement with Tajik and American values. Upon entering the Teahouse it is easy to become mesmerized by the colorful, intricately painted walls, but what most visitors neglect to consider is what the space means for Tajikistan and the United States. The Teahouse was gifted to Boulder at a very important time in Tajikistan's history; a time, not so long ago, when the nation was reclaiming its identity. The structure sends a different, but equally significant

Overleaf: Detail photo of coffer ornamentation. (Photo by Ethan Herrold.)

1. Lawrence Vale, *Architecture Power and National Identity.*

2. ibid.

message in Boulder that aligns with the identity of the US. Ernest Gellner, social anthropologist and philosopher, defines nationalism as a theory of political legitimacy.[1] His work explained the differences between national identity, and how external forces affected the formation of collective identity (and this marks the distinction between our discussion here with the discussion on identity in the previous essay). For Gellner, nationalism is structured by political beliefs, and the society that agrees with the majority assumes their national identity. Scholar of national identity, Lawrence Vale argues that national identity is not a natural attribute that precedes statehood but a process that must be cultivated for a long time after a regime has gained political power.[2] But not everyone subscribes to the same ideals and beliefs, and yet collective identity is formed under a premise of the identity of a majority.

The formation of identity is indicative of its relationship to an individual, yet it also has the ability to relate to the majority. Does collective identity encompass everyone's ideology? Most commonly it does not. The majority serve as stakeholders of their collective identity. As individual identity forms one's perceptions, these perceptions are appreciated on a small, personal scale. However, collective identity relates to the larger whole and is formed from the association of shared ideals. The juxtaposition between individual and collective identity assumes that the majority recognizes the same values and in return defines their national identity. These ideals are then regulated by the majority in hopes to coerce an assumed collective identity, or in other words, to be able to construct a national identity as it is formed from commonly shared ideals.

Nationalism, however, can exist without a nation state. For example, Kurdish nationalism is evident and has formed without a recognized nation. This is an apparent example of how collective identity can establish national identity. As architecture historian Muna Güvenç reflects, "Before, I didn't know that I was a Kurd. We were all Turks. As I have lived here, now I know that I am a Kurd. Kurd is my identity."[3] By creating collective community values, Kurdish nationalism was born. Kurds were able to reinforce their collective identity by establishing historical monuments. These monuments were inherent to their identity as they were able to create a relationship amongst their culture regardless of the recognition of their defined nation. This collective identity was able to evoke a sense of nationalism; a sense of unity through their identity.

Frequently, architecture can provoke a sense of national identity and nationalism. By erecting monuments that are associated with a state's ideals and values, architecture gains significance for the state. In the Kurdish example, by establishing built evidence of their identity, the structural evidence illustrates Kurdish values on a more apparent level. Ultimately this creates a physical showcase of how they perceive their identity, or more importantly how they wish to be recognized on a global level. According to Vale, objects and events, monuments and ceremonies, all contribute meaningful symbols to the production and consolidation of the 'we.'[4] These physical forms can create unity among individuals, but they also have the potential to become abrasive as not every identity is always represented. Typically, it is the identity of the political power that wants to be recognized.

3. Muna Güvenç, "Narratives of Kurdish Nationalism."

4. Lawrence J. Vale, Architecture, Power, and National Identity.

5. Lawrence J Vale. "Mediated Monuments and National Identity."

6. Shelley Egoz, "Nation, City, Place."

7. Renata Latuf de Oliveira Sanchez and Stephen Essex, "The Challenge of Urban Design."

Architecture's manifestation of national identity is an influential tool , a tool that has been utilized by governments for centuries. Lawrence Vale believes that as societies have grown larger and more complex, the built environment has been asked to clarify and reinforce diverse kinds of identities, often ones held quite tenuously.[5] According to Vale, architects have the immense responsibility of representing the numerous cultural elements that make up a nation's identity and it's no surprise that there are major political influences that force them to abandon their ethical path. Vale also argues that designers often, whether consciously or not, become agents who rein-force political agendas.[6] One example is the Olympic Games where the host city is given the opportunity to show to the entire world the image of their nation that they want people to see. In doing so, governments typically wipe their issues under the rug to avoid global embarrassment. The history of the Olympic Games has been littered with examples of extravagant facilities (that sometimes become superfluous once the Games are over).[7] In many cases, the event structures are built to impress spectators and express power, rather than being lasting monuments that citizens feel connected to.

The Teahouse was also utilized by a government, but in a more positive, constructive manner than the previous exam-ple. The Teahouse was delivered to Boulder shortly following the collapse of the USSR. Tajikistan had recently been returned to an independent nation and the country was in the critical position of reclaiming its identity. For centuries, teahouses have stood as an architectural form that speak volumes about Tajik identity. It stands as no surprise then, that when the participants of the Sisters Cities shared an expression of Tajik identity, it was manifest architecturally through the Teahouse.

But in order to fully understand what forms of national identity are expressed in the Teahouse, it is important to distinguish which elements of the Teahouse were culturally appropri-

Boulder-Dushanbe Teahouse dedication ceremony. (Photo from by BDSC archives.)

ated and determine what the driving force behind their appropriation was. At its essence, cultural appropriation is the adoption of a cultural element or aspect into a different culture than where that particular element dominated in the first place. In some cases, this refers to an element of the minority being appropriated by the majority. Most political buildings are architecturally representative of the identity of the majority. Vale reminds us that the national identity communicated through the

8. Lawrence J. Vale,
*Architecture, Power,
and National Identity.*

production of a parliament building usually highlights the identity of a dominant group within a plural society.[8] The dominant group refers to either the political majority or the cultural majority, and plural society indicates one in which there are multiple groups present.

With these ideas in mind, we think it prudent to ask if the Teahouse is an example of cultural appropriation. In Dushanbe, Tajikistan, the teahouse is an element of the culture supported by the majority of its citizens. This is evident in the number of and popularity of teahouses in Dushanbe. Thus, the national identity of teahouses in Dushanbe are representative of the national identity of Tajikistan. However, in the case of the Teahouse situated in the US and emplaced in Boulder, what happens to Tajik national identity gets a bit more complex.

For many visitors of the Teahouse, the intricate paintings, architecture, and carvings are not apparently representative of Tajikistan. This is not because they aren't doing a good job at representing Tajikistan, but rather that elements of Tajik culture are very foreign, and even uncategorizable for many visitors of the Teahouse in Boulder. One would have to be educated in the history of Central Asia or teahouses, generally, to know the association without any other indicators. However, this does not mean that the Teahouse goes unnoticed or underappreciated. The elements of design that make the Teahouse apparently unique in the context of Boulder, are the same elements of design valued in Tajikistan that make the Teahouse a part of its national identity, such as high quality of craftsmanship, and attention to detail and color. However, just because these design

Marufjon Mirakhmatov hand painting the exterior of the Dushanbe Teahouse in fall 2018. (Photo by Ethan Herrold.)

elements that are valued in Tajikistan are present in the Teahouse in Boulder does not mean they were culturally appropriated. The Teahouse in Boulder is a collaborative effort to produce a piece of architecture for the city of Boulder that is representative of Tajikistan, rather than an example of Boulder working independently to appropriate a Tajikistan teahouse, which would likely result in something very different than what the Teahouse actually is.

That said, there are some elements of the architecture of the Teahouse that reveal some dynamics of appropriation. The Dushanbe Teahouse needed to attract customers and bring in a profit. The first way to make this possible was by allowing the program to become a restaurant open all day, rather than just a place to have tea. This required the building to be locked and closed from the public as needed. In Tajikistan many of the teahouses are open to the sky in the center of the ceiling, and oftentimes without walls or doors. However, to operate as a place of business and to keep out inclement weather, a roof and doors that closed and locked were a necessity.

The purpose and design of the Teahouse were modified to fit into the national identity, cultural expectations, and the climate of Boulder. This resulted in a unique design-and-build collaboration that is representative of the national identities of

Traditional open-air teahouse in Tajikistan (Photo By Nathan Jones.)

both the US and Tajikistan. National identity does not come about easily and is always molded from what has come before.[9]

The architecture and the program of the Teahouse have elements of both Tajik and American national identity embedded within them. It possesses a hybrid identity rather than a culturally appropriated one. Design historian Javier Gimeno-Martinez tells us that the characterization of the nation can point in different directions, stressing the nation's past or its future.[10] The Dushanbe Teahouse supports this notion in its capacity as a physical manifestation of Tajikistan's effort of reconstruct and express its national identity.

Furthermore, the Teahouse supports the argument that architecture can exemplify multiple nations through the co-construction of identity. There are many American values and customs (whether celebrated or not) that are reflected in the building, the most prevalent being its appropriated, commercial function. Gimeno-Martinez also tells us that national art crystallizes the nation by presenting it in concrete form, thereby endowing it with an enduring, monumental quality.[11] Indeed, the Teahouse expresses the sense of nation and national identity vividly. Its presence in Boulder adds intrigue to its narrative. Its monumentality gives significance to its expression.

9. Lawrence J. Vale, *Architecture, Power, and National Identity.*

10. Javier Gimeno-Martinez, *Design and National Identity.*

11. Ibid.

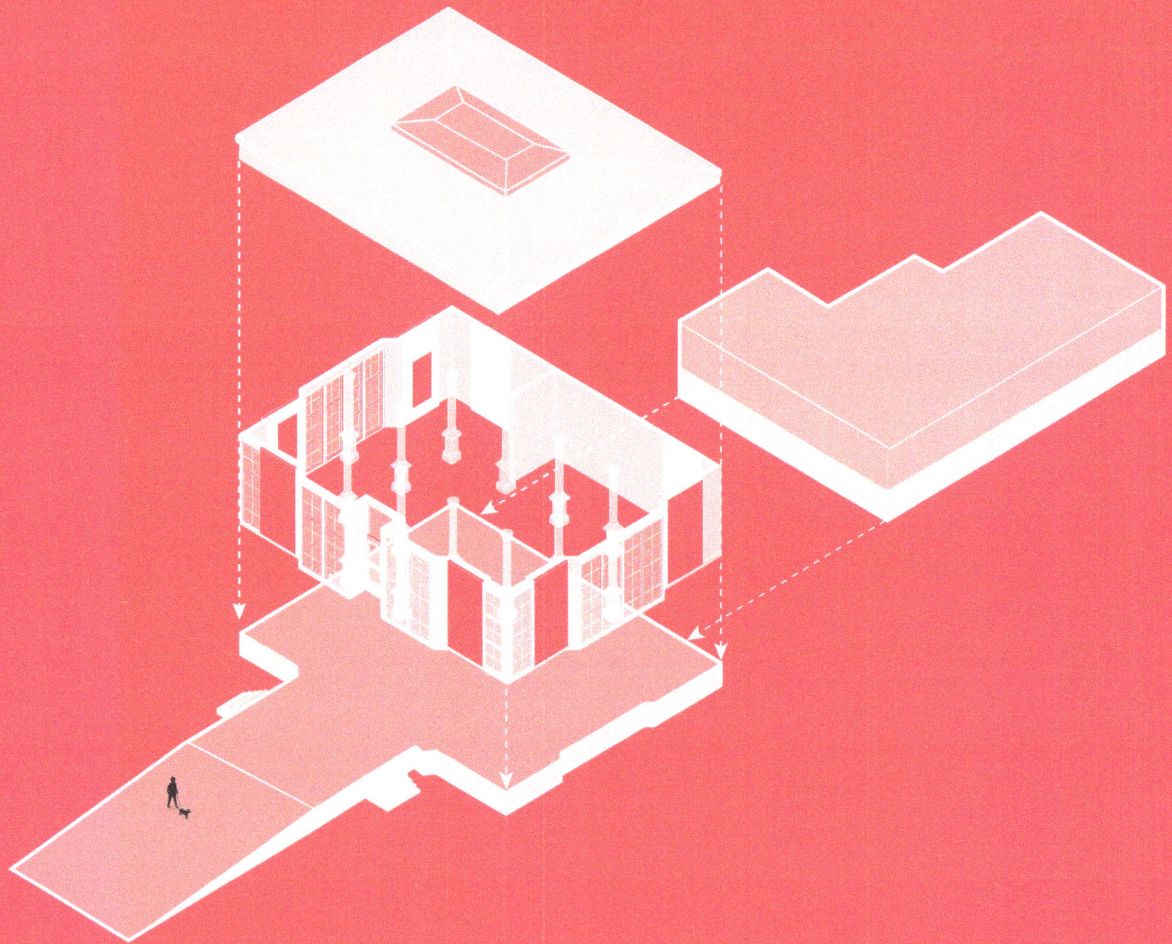

Exploded axonometric view of the Teahouse highlighting additions

Architectural Evolution

———

The Boulder Dushanbe Teahouse has experienced many modifications since the original design was completed in Tajikistan. Many of these changes are a direct result of varying cultural and climate differences including those inherent in the refashioning of the Teahouse as a restaurant. Many stakeholders took a large role in the creation, modification, and the possibility of having the teahouse in Boulder. These changes have allowed the Teahouse to serve as a popular place of leisure in Boulder and inspires an understanding of Central Asian cultures.

The Evolution of the Dushanbe Teahouse

Original Design

In 1987 the Teahouse was designed in Tajikistan as a traditional raised open-air structure, with an open roof. Inside there is a coffered painted ceiling with a central pool and statues surrounded by fourteen hand-carved wood columns (A).

Site Selection

After being assembled and disassembled in Tajikistan, the pieces of the Teahouse were shipped to Boulder and arrived in 1990. In 1991, City Council determined the Teahouse would be located on 13th Street in Boulder, just east of Central Park.

Climate Modification

In 1991 Vern Seieroe collaborated with Tajik architect, Lado Shanidze, to discuss modifications to function with Boulder's climate. They added walls, windows (B), and skylights (C), so that the Teahouse was suitable for its new intended use as a restaurant. They also modified the foundation and ramp to be ADA accessible.

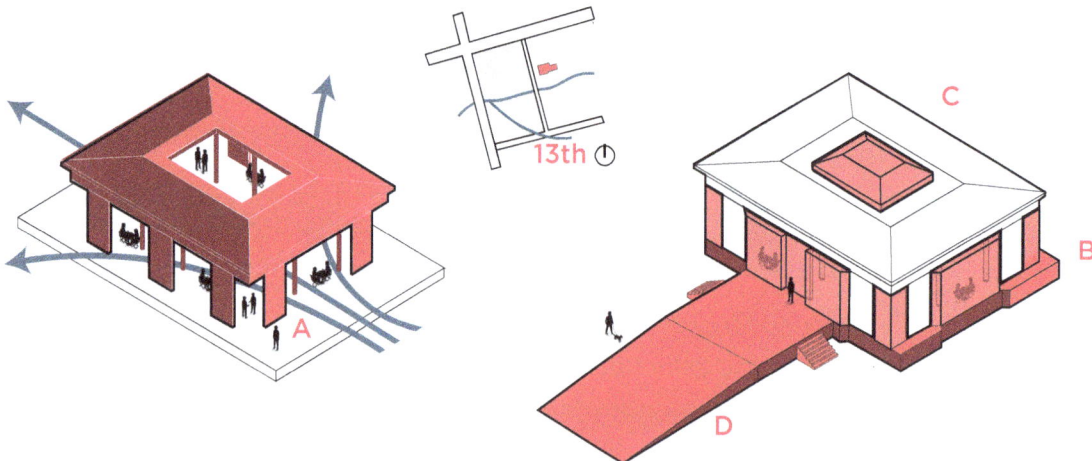

13th

Program Modifications

To function as a restaurant and comply with Boulder's building codes and safety requirements, an addition and other elements were added. The addition (E) included a commercial kitchen, office space, accessible public restrooms, as well as a ramp, designated parking, delivery access, and trash storage.

Outdoor Modifications

The Boulder-Dushanbe Sister Cities organization gifted the Teahouse with garden and additional walking paths. Rose gardens, pergolas, and outdoor seating were added (F).

Completion

The Teahouse was completed and opened in May 1998.

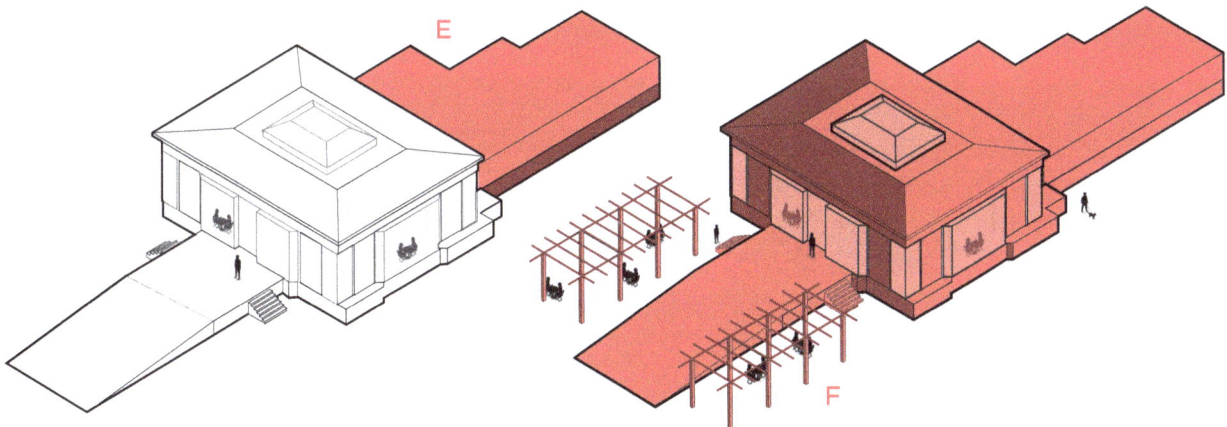

Regional Architecture as Process

Antonio Celano | Hanaan Llewellyn | Ethan Herrold

Buildings reflect space. They embody the cultural and regional values that exist across national boundaries. They respond to climatic and geographical conditions. Buildings reflect humanity.

Regionalism highlights these qualities as an architectural process. The Oxford Companion to Architecture defines regionalism in architecture as "the desire to shape buildings according to the particular characteristics of a certain place."[1] Architect and theorist (and author of this book's preface) William Bechhoefer writes that, "Regionalism requires that architecture reflect its time, place and culture and that it links the past, the present and perhaps the future."[2] The Boulder

Overleaf: Aspen, Colorado. (Photo by Ethan Herrold.)

1. Patrick Goode, "Critical Regionalism."

2. William B. Bechhoefer, *Visions of Place: Regionalism and Architecture.*

North side of the Teahouse on a snowy day. (Photo by Ethan Herrold.)

3. Patrick Goode, "Critical Regionalism."

Dushanbe Teahouse is a regional building built for a foreign place and a vastly different culture. In this essay, we consider how theories of regionalism in architecture might expand our appreciation of the Teahouse.

There are many forms of regionally inspired architecture. Vernacular and regional architecture stem from the ambition to construct buildings in response to place. Vernacular architecture represents a process of development by the collective actions of individuals. When vernacular buildings scale up from small pockets of reactive building and construction into a representational design of a location, they join the regional style of that location.[3] While both vernacular and regional architecture have geographic connotations, regional architecture defines an architectural territory that may encompass a range of vernaculars.

Regionalism, however, is a social process, a kind of place-making that bridges cultural identity, social change, environmental factors, and other characteristics of a specific place. Regional architecture, therefore, is developed by the actions and collective knowledge of interested parties local to a region over a span of time. While vernacular and regional architecture usually have their origins in informality (or "architecture without architects"), region*ist* buildings materialize as formal reactions to a given space by dedicated designers or professional architects.[4]

4. Heath, *Vernacular Architecture and Regional Design.*

The case of Boulder is instructive here. Since its earliest permanent settlement in 1858, the foreign was native to Boulder. Foreign people, ideas, cultures, and customs all flocked to the city. Its settlement as a gold rush town brought people from all over the world. It was a convenient stop along the route paralleling the South Platte river; prospectors would either stop in Boulder or continue to Denver.[5] As a uniquely cosmopolitan town, Boulder has immersed itself with a vast array of people simultaneously making it their home. Even as such, regionalism can be tracked in Boulder's architecture through, for example, building materials.

5. Lambrecht, *Boulder, 1859-1919.*

Brick buildings have characterized the architecture of Boulder since 1866 when the Dabney-Macky building was built on Pearl St. What is still available today on Pearl Street—lined with brick business—establishes the Boulder regional architectural language.[6] River rock walls have also been popular in Boulder regional architecture since 1865. The Squires-Tourtellot house on Spruce Street, for example, famously utilized

6. Ibid

them in its walls. Local river rocks were a convenient and available material, thus this form of building facade soon became part of the Boulder regional aesthetic.

Indeed, regional architecture often originates from necessity and convenience. Regional architectural elements react to local climate, geography, customs, family structures, needs, and available resources. Over time, these elements develop into tradition and lose their immediate connection with the practical. Many things over time trend toward aesthetic applications or simply become ornamental and vestigial, especially when regional values are applied outside of the original region.[7]

7. Lambrecht, *Boulder, 1859-1919*.

Simple wooden timber-framed houses were among the earliest forms of Boulder regional architecture. They typified the material used for homes where the common settler would have lived. Timber was readily available, affordable, and simple to construct. An early example of this form is the house built on the corner of 14th and Pearl in 1860 by Andrew Macky.[8]

8. Ibid.

The Boulder region also has an intimate relationship with water. Many ditches, like the Andersen ditch or the Beasley ditch, were created initially to meet the growing demands for water consumption, including supply water for agriculture. There is a large portion of Boulder regional architecture that has adapted from this interaction with water features, including these ditches and Boulder and Bear Creeks. It is common to have a small bridge at residences located on the ditches. This has led to formalized neighborhood streets today in which residences sit behind a ditch and have frontal access via a small bridge. Indeed, Boulder Creek has influenced the architecture around it. Throughout history, the creek has inspired considerable creek-front housing. However, the practicality of this housing has come into question in recent years, stemming from the devastating floods of 2013 and possible flooding in the future.

At first glance, Boulder and Dushanbe seem vastly different. Yet, in ways we find them to be very much alike. Similar to Boulder, Dushanbe houses a diversity of cultures, customs, and ethnic traditions. "Dushanbe's architecture post-independence is actant, a mnemonic and iconographic bridge between the present and favored historical periods in a quest for

9. Katherine Hughes, "From the Achaemenids to Somoni."

national origins. A bricolage of historical symbols, including those of Achaemenid Iran and the early Islamic Samanids, is displayed here in a city with Soviet foundations."[9]

Katherine Hughes argues that iconography is a key component of Tajik culture. The architecture of Tajikistan and iconography are inseparable. Symbolism, icons, imagery, and traditional form adorn Tajik regional architecture. Ornamentation through the form of iconography is paramount in the Tajik architectural language. And we feel that teahouses exemplify this.[10]

10. Ibid.

Teahouses are places of cultural communication. Much like the Boulder Dushanbe Teahouse, they are often adorned with rich iconography and symbolism. In our experience as users of the Teahouse and as architecture students investigating the Teahouse's cultural situation in Boulder, we agree with George Peknik's statement that, "the Asian teahouse is a social institution that is the center of daily life for many people (usually men) from Istanbul to Tokyo... Teahouses are to Central Asians what the Internet has become to many Americans; a place to congregate and communicate with others, have fun, and learn about what's going on in the world and in one's town."[11] As such, the regionally significant iconography that the Teahouse expresses adds a prominent and surprising characteristic to Boulder's architectural landscape. The juxtaposition of regional architectural priorities as evidenced in the adjacency of the Boulder Museum of Contemporary Art and the Teahouse produce, in our view, a stunning narrative of the power of regionalism.

11. George Peknik, *Meaning of the Boulder-Dushanbe Teahouse.*

Although the architecture of the Teahouse is neither vernacular or regional to Boulder or Dushanbe, it incorporates elements of the regional architecture as necessary adjustments to the Boulder environment. Yet, the Teahouse carries a clear sense of a foreign regionalism. And this expression is an important part of what gives it its magic. The Teahouse is an outlier in the city. Its traditional Tajik paintings and ornate sculpture simply do not integrate into Boulder's mountain-west architectural language. The Teahouse is an instant landmark due to its uniqueness. Representing a foreign vernacular, its tension with the Boulder regional architecture that surrounds it makes for a fascinating urban fabric.

Boulder Museum of Contemporary Art (Right) next to the Teahouse. (Photo by Kate Sector.)

Despite its architectural form, the Teahouse has elements of American culture ingrained in its existence. It is a place of cultural consumption and of community gathering. It has comforts typical of North American cultural and hospitality buildings: air-conditioning, a dedicated entrance, fire suppression system and alarms, a code-worthy kitchen, and efficiently spaced tables. Yet, the core of the Teahouse was constructed using traditional methods and techniques of a distant culture. Its ornamentation is so detailed and regionally rooted that foreign artisans are the only ones capable of restoring it.

We are inspired by the idea that a building is not regional simply by virtue of its location. It must be constructed by the knowledge and collective ideals of the people who design and inhabit it. The Dushanbe Teahouse, while moderately adapted, is not based on the collective ideals of Boulder residents. It more strikingly communicates our image of the ideals of Tajik people. But the architectural modifications, use, and origin story of the Teahouse complicate the traditional narrative of regionalism in architecture. We feel this is part of what makes the Teahouse such a powerful connector between regions a world apart—made adjacent by this building, how we use it, and the intricate story of its maintenance, which we were fortunate to participate in this semester.

Opposite: Stream-side dining at the Teahouse. (Photo by Kate Sector.)

Architectural Analysis

Architecture plays a critical role in creating spaces that educate users about the purpose and culture behind their designs. Over time, the Teahouse has seen many adaptations to accommodate both Tajik and North American cultural needs. The perspectives offered by Persian architectural theory help us to better understand the significance of original design moves as well as the modifications made when incorporating this building into its new cultural home. The Teahouse provides not only an incredible space to visit but also serves as a monument to an important historic moment in time. It serves as an example of design that brings together a diverse group of people to celebrate history, identity, culture, and global friendship. Analyzing and understanding its architecture helps appreciate how the celebration is achieved.

Epilogue

In shaping the content of this book, our class of Environmental Design students joined the "trans-global community" that Nate Jones signified in the Introduction as "binding together people in Colorado and Tajikistan." In the process, though, they did something more. They challenged dominant ways of thinking about design by engaging with a vastly different architectural world view.

When we study architecture in a university, students typically learn about histories and theories of architecture that are rooted firmly in modern and colonial Western and European thought. Our texts, discussions, and precedents shape a world view (an ontology) that governs how most of us see architecture's role in our lives and in our societies. As productive as this world view has been, it is problematically biased.

Recently, a number of architecture scholars have initiated attempts to "decolonize" architectural thought by confronting its colonial past, its positioning of the West versus the rest, and dismantling power relations ingrained in assumptions about architecture from other parts of the world. Through their work with Marufjon Mirakhmatov, in reading passages in Persian architectural theory and other critical texts, and in preparing the essays and the analyses that make up this book, the students embodied the important work of decolonizing architecture. We were inspired by the speed and enthusiasm with which this cohort of undergraduate design students took to very foreign ways of thinking about and doing architecture.

The class and restoration took place in the fall of 2018, a time when much political discourse was steeped in exclusion, xenophobia, and inequality. In this context particularly, the students' enthusiasm and diligence in engaging a distant "other" was powerful. Their ideas, their time with Marufjon, and their design work reflected their growing ethos of connection. Where the news told stories of walls, detention, and conflict, the students work and our Teahouse community shaped connection, expression, and understanding.

Contributors

Fall 2018 Teahouse Class

Sophie Burgess, Antonio Celano, Abigail Clark, Carley Cordrey, Jason Green, Grant Harrop, Ethan Herrold, Madison Liedtke, Hanaan Llewellyn, Josephine Phillips, Justice Ramos, Trevor Shelden, Madison Smith, Brett Sametz, Emelia Steinmetz, and Madison Wight.

Sophie Burgess has always had a passion for art and painting. She has deeply appreciated the fusion of new technical skills and historical perspectives that she acquired during her time working on the Boulder Teahouse. During university, Sophie has strived to fuel her passion for sustainability and the environment. In May she will be graduating with a Bachelors of Environmental Design specifying in Landscape Architecture along with a Certificate in Renewable and Sustainable Energy. In the future, she plans to couple her interests in sustainability, environmental policy, justice, and design to finding ecological, research-based solutions within the design field.

Antonio Celano is studying architecture to serve those around him through intentional and meaningful design. He is passionate about the essence of emotional spaces that inspire awe, beauty, and a search for truth. Through a life of learning he wants to know what spaces become spiritual homes and how his design can become ever more thoughtful, and rich with experienced depth.

Abby Clark strives to use architecture to solve the environmental problems of today and the future. She loves to travel, discover new cultures, and understand the meaning behind architecture. The Teahouse Restoration course was a way to deeply examine and discuss Tajik culture and architecture, as well as leave her mark through painting. Upon graduation Abby will continue to travel and discover new cultures through the lens of a camera, starting with a two month US road trip with her sister.

Carley Cordrey grew up in Boulder, Colorado and fostered a connection with the Dushanbe Teahouse from a young age. She is passionate about designs which promote the highest quality of life and allow culture to thrive. She is an advocate for community engagement, childhood development, and protecting our planet through sustainable design. In her free time, Carley enjoys biking, skiing, hiking, and enjoying Colorado's sunshine.

Ethan Herrold is an architecture student and photographer. He sees the world through his camera lens, seeking to capture a unique perspective—both in the world of design and in photography. His interest in historic restoration and adaptive reuse brought him to the Teahouse Restoration course. Ethan employed skills as a photographer to document both the restoration process and the completed artwork at the Boulder Teahouse. He will pursue a career in photography upon graduating in May 2019.

Grant Harrop is currently studying architecture in hopes of fostering community growth and promoting a lifestyle that utilizes design as a means to create meaningful spaces. He hopes to one day start his own development firm and have the ability to establish connections across the world. In his free time, he enjoys making new experiences while traveling and creating memories with his friends and family.

Nate Jones is an applied anthropologist interested in how state policies, institutions, and personal relationships influence the production of nationalized and ethnicized artistic and architectural projects in Tajikistan and Uzbekistan. His research focuses on the formation of urban precincts and the linkages between formal and informal organizations in Central Asian cities. Nate serves on the board of directors for Boulder Dushanbe Sister Cities and assisted with organizing the restoration of the Dushanbe Teahouse to which this book is dedicated.

Madison Liedtke is an aspiring designer for a multitude of trades. She has always enjoyed architecture, interior design, graphic design, and studio arts. She is highly motivated to create space that has a heavy artistic meaning and sparks a connection with its users. She has yet to decide if she will become a licensed architect but in the meantime, she will be conceptually designing for a local Denver residential architecture firm where she will be gaining creative experience with both architecture and interior design. She hopes to continue this full time after graduation in May 2019.

Josephine Phillips has many passions when it comes to design: architecture, sustainable practices, building restoration, acoustic design, and art installation are just a few. She spent her time in the Environmental Design program collecting exciting and unique experiences, such as the Dushanbe Teahouse class, in hopes that they will set a course for an equally unique and exciting career for her in the design world.

Shawhin Roudbari uses his research and teaching to bring attention to ways architects and planners take on contentious political issues through their work, their institutions, and as part of social movements. Through his work, he hopes to empower design professionals to help shape the built environment in ways that further equity and justice. Shawhin is an assistant professor in Environmental Design at the University of Colorado Boulder.

Brett Sametz did not consider himself a painter prior to the Teahouse restoration project. In fact, he still doesn't, but has obtained a new appreciation for the art through the countless hours spent practicing Tajik technique. Although Brett is not going to be a professional painter, he hopes to use his passion for design to create works that make people realize how beautiful and obtainable sustainability can be. After graduating from CU, Brett plans on joining an interior architecture firm in Denver.

Kate Sector is a recent graduate from the Program of Environmental Design. Kate has always been fascinated by the Boulder Dushanbe Teahouse. Never did she imagine she would be a co-editor on a publication about the building, both helping to create the book and producing the architectural analysis and diagrams on the Teahouse. In addition to historic preservation, Kate's passion lies in sustainable practices and consulting within architecture. After graduation, Kate will join the architecture firm, Lake Flato, in San Antonio, Texas.

Trevor Shelden is an environmental designer and has aspirations of running an architecture & design-build firm. Growing up in the mountains of Colorado he has been inspired by the astonishing planet we live in today, driving his passion for energy and sustainability. In his free time, Trevor enjoys art, soccer, skiing, camping, and adventuring. After graduating in May, Trevor is traveling across Southeast Asia and then moving to Southern California to start work at an architecture & design-build firm.

Maddie Smith is obtaining a degree in Environmental Design and is emphasizing in architecture. Her interest in architecture history is what drew her to the Teahouse Restoration course. Future plans after finishing her degree include traveling to different countries, gathering inspiration from different cultures and styles of architecture to use in her practice one day.

Emelia Steinmetz's fascination and passion in all things design, specifically interior design, lead her to the restoration course and the Teahouse. She strives to create a better world and believes much of that can come from design. After graduating from the University of Colorado Boulder with a degree in Environmental Design in May of 2019, she hopes to chase her dream of becoming an interior designer. Although this is the current plan, she is open to whichever direction her life will take her knowing she will have a positive impact no matter what.

Opposite: Learning floral motifs with Marufjon Mirakhmatov. (Photo by Ethan Herrold.)

Bibliography

Ardalan, Nader and Laleh Bakhtiar. *The Sense of Unity: the Sufi Tradition in Persian Architecture.* Built Environment Publishing, 2016.

Bechhoefer, William B. "Visions of Place: Regionalism and Architecture." Ismet Odabaşio and School of Architecture, Planning and Preservation, University of Maryland, 2010.

Bourdieu, Pierre. *Outline of a Theory of Practice.* Cambridge, UK: Cambridge University Press, 1977.

Broadbent, Geoffrey. *Design in Architecture: Architecture and the Human Sciences.* London: John Wiley and Sons Inc, 1973.

Buchman, Barbara. *Boulder Dushanbe Teahouse.* Carnegie Library, 1998.

Cartwright, Mark, "Pantheon." Ancient History Encyclopedia, 09 April 2018.

Charles Correa. "Quest for Identity," *Architecture and Identity,* 1983.

Creighton, Thomas H. *The Architecture of Monuments: The Franklin Delano Roosevelt Memorial Competition.* New York: Reinhold Pub. Corp, 1962.

Egoz, Shelley. "Nation, City, Place: Rethinking Nationalism." *Landscape Review*, 11:2 (2007): 57-59.

Flowers, Jeff. "Evaporative Coolers: How They Differ From Other A/C Units." *Compact Appliance*, 15 (2017).

Gimeno-Martinez, Javier. *Design and National Identity.* London: Bloomsbury Academic, 2016.

Eldemery, Ibrahim Mostafa. Globalization Challenges in Architecture." *Journal of Architectural & Planning Research*, 26:4 (2009): 343-54.

Goode, Patrick. "Critical Regionalism." *The Oxford Companion to Architecture.* Oxford University Press, 2009.

Güvenç, Muna. "Constructing a Narrative of Kurdish Nationalism in the Urban Space of Diyarbakir, Turkey." *Traditional Dwellings and Settlements Review* 23:1 (2011): 25-40

Harada, Jiro, and C. Geoffrey Holme. "The lesson of Japanese architecture." *Milton Keynes: Studio*, 2011.

Hauge, Åshild Lappegard. "Identity and Place: A Critical Comparison of Three Identity Theories," *Architectural Science Review*, 50:1 (2007): 44-51.

Heath, Kingston. *Vernacular Architecture and Regional Design.* London: Routledge, 2009.

Heathcote, Edwin. *Monument Builders, Modern Architecture and Death.* New York, Academy Editions, 1999.

Ho, Engseng. T*he Graves of Tarim: Genealogy and Mobility across the Indian Ocean.* Berkeley, CA: University of California Press, 2006.

Hughes, Katherine. *From the Achaemenids to Somoni: National Identity and Iconicity in the Landscape of Dushanbe's Capitol Complex.* Central Asian Survey, 2017.

Huyssen, Andreas. "Monument and Memory in a Postmodern Age." *Yale Journal of Criticism,* 6 (1993): 249–61.

Knight, Cher Krause and Harriet F. Senie (ed.s). *A Companion to Public Art.* In Blackwell Companions to Art History (Book 11), New York: Wiley-Blackwell, 2016.

Lambrecht, Mona. *Boulder, 1859-1919.* Charleston, SC: Arcadia Publishing, 2008.

Latuf de Oliveira Sanchez, Renata and Stephen Essex. "The Challenge of Urban Design in Securing Post-Event Legacies of Olympic Parks." *Journal of Urban Design*, 23:2 (2018): 278-297.

Mahgoub, Yasser. "Architecture and the expression of cultural identity in Kuwait," *The Journal of Architecture,* 12:2 (2007): 165-182.

Morby, Alice. "Adjaye's African American History Museum Wins Design of the Year 2017," *Dezeen*, January 28, 2018.

Nomer, Nedim. "Ziya Gökalp's Idea of Cultural Hybridity." *British Journal of Middle Eastern Studies*, 44:3 (2017): 408-428.

Osborne, James F. "Counter-Monumentality and the Vulnerability of Memory." *Journal of Social Archaeology*, 17:2 (2017): 163-187.

Peknik, George. T*he Meaning of the Boulder-Dushanbe Teahouse: the Inspiring Story of an Architectural Gem, a Gift from Dushanbe, Tajikistan, to Its American Sister City, Boulder, Colorado*: Hoopoe Publications, 2004.

Proshansky, Harold M. "The City and Self-Identity." *Environment and Behavior,* 10:2 (June 1978): 147–69.

Ramsey, Lara and Kathryn Barth. "Boulder-Dushanbe Teahouse. Boulder, Colorado." *Historic Context and Survey Prepared for the City of Boulder, Colorado*. October 2010.

Rapoport, Amos. *House, Form and Culture*. Prentice-Hall, (1969).

Renan, Ernestand and Charles Beard. *Lectures on the Influence of the Institutions: Thought and Culture of Rome, on Christianity and the Development of the Catholic Church.* Eugene, Oregon: Wipf & Stock, 2006.

Sills, David L. "Identity." In *International Encyclopedia of the Social Sciences*, 2nd ed., Edited by William A. Darity, Jr., 551-555. Vol. 3. Detroit, MI: Macmillan Reference, 2008.

Stevens, Quentin, Karen A. Franck, and Ruth Fazakerley. "Counter-monuments: the anti-monumental and the dialogic." *The Journal of Architecture*, 23:5 (2018): 718-739.

Three Leaf Concepts. "A symbol of Peace and Global Friendship." Boulder Dushanbe Teahouse, Three Leaf Concepts, 2019.

Timmermann, Achim. "Memory and Redemption: Public Monuments and the Making of Late Medieval Landscape." *Journal of the Society of Architectural Historians,* 8 (2017).

Treib, Marc. *Spatial Recall: Memory in Architecture and Landscape.* London: Routledge, 2009.

Tylor, Edward B. *Anthropology: An introduction to the Study of Man and Civilization.* New York: D. Appletion, 1909.

Unwin, Simon. *Analysing Architecture.* Routledge, 2014.

World Trade Press. *Tajikistan Society & Culture Complete Report: An All-Inclusive Profile Combining All of Our Society and Culture Reports.* Petaluma: World Trade Press, 2010.

Vale, Lawrence J. *Architecture, Power, and National Identity.* London: Routledge, 2014.

Vale, Lawrence J. "Mediated Monuments and National Identity." *The Journal of Architecture*, 4:4 (1999): 391-408.

Verdery, Katherine. T*he Vanishing Hectare: Property and Value in Post-Socialist Romania.* Ithaca, NY: Cornell University Press, 2004.

Opposite: exterior ceramic tile. (Photo by Ethan Herrold.)

www.ingramcontent.com/pod-product-compliance
Lightning Source LLC
Chambersburg PA
CBHW042047090426
42733CB00039B/2657